40 YEARS

Angelo Van Bogart

07-2044

©2007 Krause Publications

Published by

700 East State Street • Iola, WI 54990-0001
715-445-2214 • 888-457-2873
www.krausebooks.com

Our toll-free number to place an order or obtain
a free catalog is (800) 258-0929.

Library of Congress Control Number: 2007922996

ISBN-13: 978-0-89689-568-3
ISBN-10: 0-89689-568-8

Designed by Elizabeth Krogweld
Edited by Joe Kertzman

Printed in China

On the Cover
Among the 16 original Hot Wheels cars was the Custom Cougar, shown here in orange. All Hot Wheels cars from the inaugural line are collectible, but collectors particularly seek out the Custom Cougar for its good looks and faithfulness to Mercury's muscle car. The Custom Cougar shown on the cover is from the collection of Tom Michael. (Robert Best cover photo)

Dedication: To my brother Nathan, who not only collects Hot Wheels cars, but also loves playing with them.

Acknowledgments:

Hot Wheels cars are fun, and working with Hot Wheels cars should be just as fun. Thanks to the great people who helped assemble this book, writing it was as enjoyable as sending a freshly opened First Edition down a stretch of orange track.

If it weren't for collector Bob Whaley, the dazzling Spectraflame® colors of Hot Wheels cars wouldn't be illustrated in this book. Whaley opened his collection to Doug Mitchel's camera lens and my own curiosity. For Whaley's time and gift of sharing his collection, I am deeply indebted to him. To complement Whaley's collection and my own in this book, my fellow F&W Publications coworker Tom Michael generously allowed his childhood redline collection to be photographed, and even dragged them out of his home in sub-zero temperatures for our photo shoot.

Several Mattel staffers also took time out of their busy schedules, and continue to do so through my Hot Wheels column in *Toy Cars & Models* magazine, to share the constantly changing history of the Hot Wheels brand. For their patience and valuable efforts to share Hot Wheels information, I offer a since "Thank you." Those Mattel employees include, but are not limited to, Mark Jones, Ray Adler, John Ludwig and Phil Riehlman.

Toy Cars & Models Editor Merry Dudley and *Toy Shop* Editor Tom Bartsch have also come to my aid by editing my Hot Wheels column and encouraging my fascination with toys, as well as my professionalism in the publishing field. On this project, book editor Joe Kertzman showed a level of patience that is unheard of in a deadline-riddled publishing schedule, and his efforts to pour over this story are deeply appreciated.

Finally, this book would not contain the beautiful photographs it does if it weren't for the efforts of Doug Mitchel, Kris Kandler and Bob Best. Thanks to their skills, the pages between the covers show the excitement that Hot Wheels cars created for generations of children across the planet.

Contents

Introduction

40 years of hot designs and cool collectibles

In 1968, when Hot Wheels cars hit the market, toy manufacturers didn't expect new toys to catch the fancy of children for more than a year. If a toy's popularity went to two years, it was considered to have a long life. But for 40 years, children have sought out Hot Wheels cars, cracked them open from their packages, and rolled them around linoleum kitchen floors and living room carpets. For just as long, collectors have raided store shelves for the die-cast toy cars and displayed them like valuable vases and other works of art, and rightly so.

This book explains the magic of Hot Wheels cars through the eyes of someone who, like many collectors, begged his parents for Hot Wheels cars as a kid and grew into an adult collector. The creators of Hot Wheels cars, the marketing agents behind the brand and the designers are all part of the magic, and many of them explain the cars and the processes that make that magic.

Of course, Hot Wheels magic manifests itself in the form of the $1 cars that are the mainstay of the line. The cars come in many styles, including redlines, "Treasure Hunts," variations and other desirable Hot Wheels series. In each series are cars that children have enjoyed playing with and collectors have coveted since 1968.

Elliot and Ruth Handler probably never realized the longevity of the toy they had created to compete with Matchbox® cars, nor could they have predicted how much their toys would dominate the die-cast toy car market. And 40 years later, children and collectors would be hard-pressed to imagine a world without them.

Chapter One

BUILDING BETTER WHEELS

This red Custom Firebird helped set Hot Wheels sales on fire at the debut of the scale cars.

Tens of millions of children came close to missing the chance to play with Hot Wheels cars. And many adults almost lost the opportunity to build a hobby around toy cars. But thanks to the instincts of Mattel cofounder Elliot Handler, generations of young boys and girls filled their short summers racing die-cast cars down stretches of sidewalk and sections of orange racetrack.

In 1966 Handler, despite coming relatively late into the game, realized that there was room in the market for another pocket-sized, die-cast toy car. His marketing department, as well as his wife, Ruth, disagreed with his analysis. They argued that the die-cast toy car market was saturated, main-

ly by highly successful toy cars from the British Matchbox brand. Not to be stopped, Elliot trusted his instincts and set the stage for what would become Hot Wheels cars.

To compete with the highly successful Matchbox and American Tootsietoy cars, Elliot knew that his product had to be different, and better. He also knew that he couldn't do it alone, so he employed Fred Adickes, who was a member of the Chrysler design team. One of Adickes' first items

Harry Bentley Bradley was the first Hot Wheels designer on staff, and the car he drove daily, an Alexander Brothers customized 1964 El Camino, was the inspiration for how the company designed toy models of popular full-size cars of the time. The Custom Fleetside, pictured here, sported the same customizing features— a domed hood scoop with carburetor stacks, passenger car roof and redline tires—as Bradley's El Camino, but the basis was Chevrolet's 1967 C-10 Fleetside full-size truck. (Tom Michael collection)

Like all of the original 16 Hot Wheels cars, the Custom Fleetside was offered in several colors, including purple, one of the most coveted colors among children. (Tom Michael collection)

of business was to assemble a creative staff to work on designs for the proposed toy, and he advertised a design position in the Detroit Free Press. The advertisement attracted Harry Bentley Bradley, a General Motors stylist working in the Cadillac studio, who accepted the position with Mattel.

Bradley was a perfect fit, although it didn't appear so initially. While at General Motors, Bradley had become known for drawing hot rods with beautiful women posed next to them. He also drove a 1964 Chevrolet El Camino hot rod, which had been customized by Detroit's famous Alexander Brothers.

Once working within Mattel's walls, Bradley began sketching away, with Elliot watching over his shoulder. The designs were not like anything Elliot had seen before, nor did they convey the vision he had in mind for his new die-cast cars.

Typically, sketches of toys under development within Mattel included children playing with accurate renderings of the toys, not the highly stylized works Bradley created. Elliot shared his feelings towards Bradley's work, but was unable to articulate what it was he sought. He just knew the die-cast cars had to be different.

Light blue makes for an attractive and desirable Spectraflame color. Here, it dresses a Custom Camaro.

This red Custom Camaro sports the much-desired door lines and outlined trunk lid.

Many consider the Custom Camaro to be the first Hot Wheels car offered. By anyone's count, this car certainly was among the first castings to be released, and in a dizzying amount of variations. Some Custom Camaros have black roofs and some have outlined doors and trunk lids. Add in the variations associated with Hong Kong versus United States production (larger taillights and a steering wheel molded in the interior tub on U.S. castings), and picking up every version becomes a challenge.

With the luxury of being able to look back at that time period, the task of creating an unusual toy car for the American market should not have been a difficult proposition.

Other die-cast car companies, including Matchbox and Corgi, were based in Europe, and their toy cars were often unrecognizable to American children. Rovers, NSU models and Leylands constituted the competition's die-cast toy lineups, and even when there was a toy car with a recognizable name, like Ford, it was a European Cortina, Zephyr or Anglia model.

American children who wanted to collect and play with cars like those in their parents' driveways had to turn to Tootsietoy. While these children could find Tootsietoy Chevrolets and Plymouths at their local Ben Franklin or Woolworth stores, the castings were simple in construction with relatively crude one-piece bodies, two axles and four wheels.

The black top on this Custom Camaro provides a contrast to its blue paint. The original owner of this Custom Camaro actually wishes he could have found an example without a black top, but Hot Wheels cars were so in demand, he picked up whatever version of the very popular and hard-to-find Custom Camaro he could. And he's glad he did today. (Tom Michael collection)

Due to its accuracy and the lack of availability of the late 1960s Plymouth Barracuda in scale form, the Custom Barracuda remains a popular redline from 1968. This blue example was built in the United States, a detail easy to pick out, thanks to the short hood scoops. (Tom Michael collection)

On a Roll?

Not all of the first Hot Wheels cars were based on the latest cars to come from Detroit and Kenosha. Ed "Big Daddy" Roth's Beatnik Bandit hit the pegs late in 1967 for the inaugural Hot Wheels 1968 run. (Tom Michael collection)

What the toys from both sides of the Atlantic Ocean had in common is that they didn't roll well. To get movement out of the cars, children had to constantly force the metal or plastic wheels to turn around the relatively large-diameter axles.

During the 1960s, when drag racing was in full bloom and muscle cars were at the starting lines of every American drag way, children aspired to recreate their own Christmas tree (drag racing) competitions on mom's kitchen floor. Yet, they couldn't duplicate realistic race action with toy cars because the scale models rolled sideways, often flipping, and just plain didn't go far.

Working under the edict that Mattel die-cast cars would have "true play value," and aware of the shortcomings of Tootsietoy, Matchbox and other

scale vehicles, Mattel engineers set out to make the new cars roll better.

One of those engineers was Jack Malek, who had already experimented with using mandolin string in toy instruments. Malek realized the potential the thin string would have in low-friction applications and suggested that it could be used to make the wheels of toy cars spin fast and smooth. Engineer Howard Newman took the principles of the low-friction wire further and developed a straight-axle suspension that allowed the cars to bounce like real cars, yet roll smoothly on the mandolin wire.

The formula for slippery-spinning wheels included the wheels themselves. Each one had a small contact area with the string, and also received a set

of bearings made of Delrin™, a plastic material from DuPont that was strong and had low-friction qualities. Most importantly, from an aesthetic view, were the red stripes on each "mag"-style wheel. The red lines became the most recognizable trait of early Hot Wheels cars.

In each step along the way, Mattel tested its development of Hot Wheels cars with children. Groups of school kids were given prototype Mattel cars and competitors' toy cars to play with, and at the end of each play session, the children were questioned as to which cars they wanted to keep. Inevitably, their choices were the prototype cars from Mattel, and the company knew it was on the right path.

Designers and engineers used these tests to gather input. During one of the sessions, children in the test group noticed that Newman's initial straight-axle setup didn't allow the toy cars to handle like real, full-size automobiles. So, Newman went back to the drawing board and came up with a fully independent torsion-bar suspension that allowed each wheel to bounce and fall independently from the other wheels. The suspension was so unusual that it was awarded a patent. Mattel had a winner.

In the meantime, Bradley continued to struggle with the design direction of the cars, but was eventually able to capture Handler's vision. As it turned out, the design Handler envisioned was a toy car that looked like Bradley's customized El Camino. What Handler sought was literally within Bradley's reach everyday as he commuted to Mattel's headquarters. And he didn't even know it.

In the early years of Hot Wheels production, castings were built in the United States and Hong Kong, resulting in differences among otherwise-identical castings. The light blue Custom Barracuda is a U.S.-built casting, identifiable by the hood scoops, which do not stretch to the back of the hood, as well as the steering wheel and dashboard molded as part of the interior tub. The copper Custom Barracuda is a Hong Kong-manufactured car with longer hood scoops and a black steering wheel that is molded separately from the interior.

The World's Greatest Muscle Cars

Not every Spectraflame color is bright and flashy. Some castings are olive or brown, like the Custom Corvette pictured here. This color on the Custom Corvette is, by far, the most valuable.

Bradley went to work drawing the day's greatest muscle cars—Mustangs, Camaros and Firebirds—while giving them customized looks that reflected those popular in southern California.

Elliot later recalled that the very same El Camino inspired a certain name that has become a part of the American vernacular. Upon seeing the El Camino, Elliot commented that Bradley's vehicle was a set of "hot wheels." Before that, the working title had been California Customs, which eventually became a recurring series. But it was "Hot Wheels" that earned the name of Mattel's wild little cars, and appropriately so.

Making the first Hot Wheels cars into muscle cars also made a lot of sense. Their fast looks would match the performance of Newman's chassis, and it put every child in the driver's seat of the cars their older brothers or influential neighbor kids were driving to school.

Mattel's cars had a twist, however. These muscle cars sported sweet rakes, aggressive hood scoops and some even featured side exhaust systems—not what you'd find on the Camaros and Mustangs at the local dealership. But you would find such features on Bradley's El Camino and other tweaked machines driven by the hot rod crowd.

Mattel beat Chevrolet's secretly guarded, new-for-1968 Corvette to market with its Custom Corvette, which ruffled a few feathers inside of Detroit. Because some Mattel designers had come from Detroit's styling studios, one of them was afforded a view of the upcoming Corvette. The Hot Wheels designer turned this casting out from memory.

Beatnik Bandit hit the line for the 1968 model year and lasted through 1971, thanks to its widespread popularity.

When it comes to shopping for a full-size car, many people skip by Mercury's Cougar and get into the driver's seat of a Ford Mustang, but Mattel didn't ignore the cool cat. The Custom Cougar was built in both the United States and Hong Kong, and with the usual amount of variations between plants. The most noticeable difference between cars built on opposite sides of the Pacific Ocean is wider taillights on Hong Kong versions. This red version without a black vinyl top is among the most sought-after versions of the casting. (Tom Michael collection)

Mattel called the paint color on the Custom Cougar "lime," but collectors now call this hue "anti-freeze." No matter what it's called, the color brings out the sculpted lines of the Custom Cougar.

When Handler told Bradley he wanted his new die-cast cars to be like the yellow El Camino, he meant it down to the color. Hot Wheels cars needed exciting hues to match their fast looks. Other die-casts from Matchbox and Tootsietoy featured reds and yellows, but the hues and luster of Hot Wheels luminescent candy colors would make the enamel colors primitive.

The magic recipe behind Hot Wheels colors went beyond the paint—it went below—right down to the metal. Rather than spray a thick coat of enamel onto the metal, the method of applying candy colors onto bare zinc alloy bodies allowed the paints to sing. The shiny, bare-metal bodies formed the base for the transparent paint, leaving a vibrant finish worthy of its own name—Spectraflame.

To hide the wild, new toys in cardboard boxes would have been criminal. Matchbox was famous for little blue-and-yellow boxes that hid the cars inside, only touting the contents through artist renderings on the sides. Instead, Mattel wisely marketed the new cars in packages that shouted the contents through clear-plastic bubbles adhered to flat, cardboard backings. The packages also received blood-rushing designs worthy of the little cars they held.

Rick Irons was responsible for designing the package, and it was he who gave it flair by avoiding a rectangular shape. Instead, he favored a wave of licking flame to top off the card. The card's die-cut shape also harmonized with the flame design, which was borrowed from the hot rod and custom

Each Hot Wheels car was offered in a blister pack with a metal collector's button, which has value beyond that of the casting. The packaging itself was revolutionary in that it could be displayed on a shelf or from a peg, although some were merely tossed into bins. Finding a blister pack without the hole for the peg broken, as it is on this Custom Eldorado's package, is particularly difficult.

Two of the most sought-after versions of Custom Firebird are pictured here in brown and light blue. Collectors also seek out the less-common Custom Firebirds that have their doors outlined.

Custom Firebirds with matching interiors are particularly sought, and this rare combination is mostly seen with red and blue. There are a few brown-on-brown Custom Firebirds, and since the color itself is not commonly found on any Custom Firebird, this example is particularly desirable.

movement that swept the nation, and California in particular, in the 1950s.

There was a method to Irons' madness. Before Hot Wheels, the working name for the die-cast cars was California Customs. When the name Hot Wheels was finalized, Irons' flamed card was a perfect match. Each cardboard backing was perfectly matched to stylized illustrations of non-descript cars by Otto Kuhni, a freelance artist who continues to design packaging for Hot Wheels collector cars.

Mattel's marketing innovation didn't end there. Handler further insisted that each package, or blis-

ter pack, not only be capable of hanging from a metal peg, but also to stand on its own. Shelf space in retail stores has always been at a premium, and it was pure genius that Handler dictate that the cars be packaged for multiple methods of display. This guaranteed Hot Wheels cars could be displayed, regardless of the type of space a Kmart or Ben Franklin store had available.

In less than a year, the Hot Wheels package had finally come together, and it was different and better, two things that were just as Elliot had planned. And not a child in the land had a clue as to what was about to hit them.

The Camaro in the 1968 Hot
Wheels lineup was joined
by its Pontiac counterpart,
the Firebird, in the toy's first
year. Bradley's modifications
to GM's Firebird earned
this casting a new name:
Custom Firebird. (Tom
Michael collection)

Some Hot Wheels cars left
the assembly line with black
roofs, and some without, but
when it came to the Custom
Eldorado, every one of
them featured the black-top
treatment. This casting of a
personal luxury coupe proves
not every Hot Wheels model
from the first year was based
on a muscle car or street rod.

The first Hot Wheels cars to debut in 1968*

Beatnik Bandit	Custom Cougar	Custom Mustang	Ford J-Car
Custom Barracuda	Custom Eldorado	Custom T-Bird	Hot Heap
Custom Camaro	Custom Firebird	Custom Volkswagen	Python
Custom Corvette	Custom Fleetside	Deora	Silhouette

Each car is identified on the following pages.

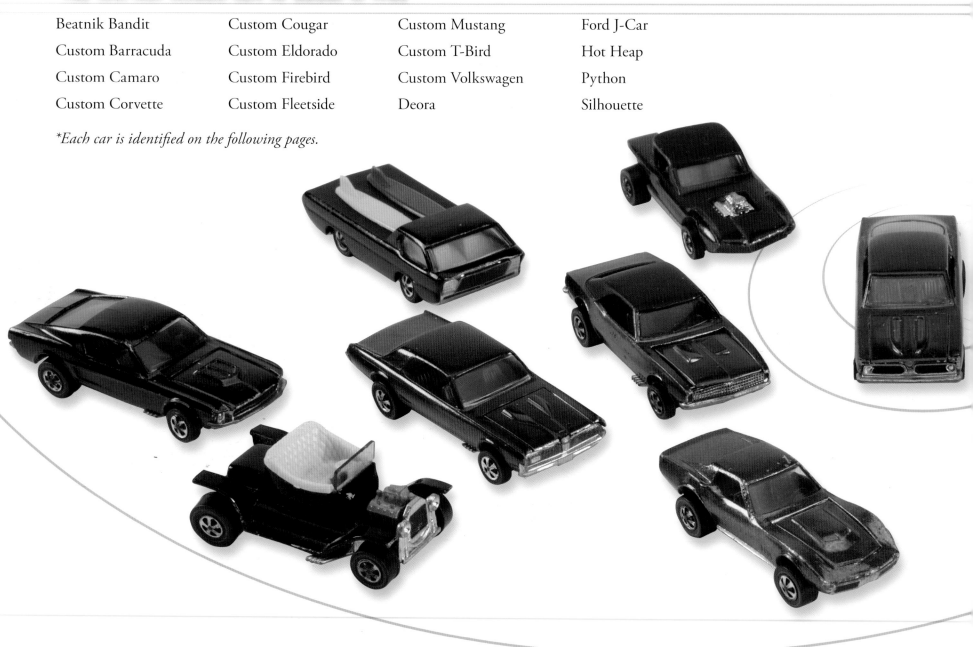

Here they are, Mattel's inaugural run of Hot Wheels cars that lit the toy market on fire and created a toy brand that is still going strong after 40 years. These Spectraflame beauties represent the "Sweet Sixteen" from 1968. (Tom Michael collection)

While the Custom Mustang is not a rare casting, there are certainly rare variations of it in existence. Versions with louvered rear windows in orange, light green and light blue are known to exist, as are Custom Mustangs with open hood scoops in gold and red. This red version is a rare open-hood-scoop model, while the gold example sports the more common sealed hood.

The Thunderbird was a personal luxury car for nights on the town and jaunts to the country club. In copper, and with a black top, the Custom T-Bird fit the image, while the hood scoop, redlines and side-exiting exhaust pipes added the hot rod flavor Harry Bradley was going for. This casting, like many others, can be found with and without the black roof and with or without outlined doors and trunks.

Volkswagens are popular in the Hot Wheels line, and the Custom Volkswagen is no exception. The light blue casting pictured is a U.S. version, easily identified by the headlights, which have been cast as part of the body. Hong Kong versions have holes in the body through which the cast-in-base headlights poke through, and European versions of the car have no sunroof.

A rose-color Custom Volkswagen features the hallmarks of a Hong Kong-built version, most notable in the headlamps, which are formed as part of the bare chassis and poke through the fenders.

For two years, children could own a Mustang of their very own with the Custom Mustang, which was based on the striking 1967 Mustang fastback. This casting is not rare, but it's certainly in demand by collectors.

Three years after Ford debuted it, the Mustang was still hot. Mattel capitalized on that popularity and gave kids what they wanted by offering the Custom Mustang. A dark blue example is pictured here. (Tom Michael collection)

One of the most popular versions of Custom T-Bird was the aqua version, pictured here. (Tom Michael collection)

Like many other Hot Wheels cars from 1968, the Deora was built in the United States and Hong Kong. This purple beauty is a U.S.-built Deora, obvious by the bare metal section between the headlights.

Even though it was a luxury car, Cadillac's Fleetwood Eldorado didn't escape from the hot rod look Harry Bradley applied to every Detroit-based 1968 casting. The Custom Eldorado received a set of exhaust pipes poking out from under the front fender, a soon-to-be-famous rake, and power bulges on the hood. This example of the Custom Eldorado wears a coat of "anti-freeze" green paint.

Harry Bradley paid homage to the Detroit-based builders of his own El Camino that he drove daily by including the Deora in the first line of Hot Wheels cars. The Alexander Brothers built the Deora as a show vehicle for Chrysler Corp. Much to Bradley's dismay, Hot Wheels creator Elliot Handler wanted the casting to sport surfboards to increase play value since the car didn't feature an opening hood. Handler got what he wanted, and Bradley was pleased with the outcome.

The Deora wasn't the only prototype to hit 1968 Hot Wheels line—the Ford J-Car prototype race machine was also part of the action. Carroll Shelby raced the full-size version of this car, but it hasn't affected the car's value among collectors.

The Ford J-Car sports many firsts: stickers, a rear-opening hood and status as the first Hot Wheels racecar. (Tom Michael collection)

Another famous hot rod to join Hot Wheels cars was the Hot Heap. The car was based on the Oakland Roadster Show "America's Most Beautiful Roadster" award-winning Model T hot rod of Don Tognotti.

Sure, there were a lot of
muscle cars in the Hot
Wheels line, but there were
a few custom gems, including
the Silhouette, pictured here
in an "anti-freeze" color.
(Tom Michael collection)

One of the most popular but
least valuable Hot Wheels
castings from 1968 is the
Silhouette. It's not because
the toy version of the
Bill Cushenbery-designed
show car is unpopular, it's
because it's so popular
nearly every kid had one.

The *Car Craft* magazine staff dreamed it up in 1961, Bill Cushenbery built it in 1963 and Mattel downsized it to fit in a pocket in 1968. The full-size version of this model was known as the Car Craft Dream Rod, but Hot Wheels called it Cheetah. Its name was immediately changed to Python, most likely because Chevrolet-powered racecars also owned the name, but a few versions snuck out with Cheetah on their bases.

The Python debuted in 1968 and lasted until 1971 in the Hot Wheels lineup. (Tom Michael collection)

Chapter Two

PREPARING FOR THE PEGS

Another truck-type casting to receive cargo was the Seasider of 1970. The bed of this Howard Rees-designed casting carried a two-tone red and white plastic boat. Although it looks similar to the Custom Fleetside and Sky Show Fleetside, the casting was completely new.

Hot Wheels cars' engineered suspensions and wheel bearings guaranteed that the cars were different and better than those of the competition. Wild paint colors and brilliant packaging made Hot Wheels cars more exciting than anything else available and ensured the cars would sell. But it wasn't an easy pitch for Elliot Handler to make inside Mattel.

From the beginning, Ruth Handler believed that Lesney's Matchbox cars had already cornered the toy car market. Elliot hoped to produce 15 million Hot Wheels cars in the first year. Ruth, on the other hand, wanted to cap Mattel's losses and keep production down to the 5-million-car mark. And it wasn't a bad idea.

Because of the constantly changing trends in the toy industry, manufacturers typically planned for a toy to pay for its research, development and production in the first year. A fickle market wouldn't guarantee interest beyond one year. If a toy maintained interest through several seasons beyond the first, it was that much more profitable.

What she, and even Elliot, didn't realize was that the exciting new Hot Wheels line would grow the interest and the market for pocket-sized cars beyond their wildest dreams.

As one of Mattel's purely original castings from 1969, Twin Mill has played an important role in the company's anniversaries, beginning with the 25th in 1993. The Twin Mill even reversed the typical pattern for die-cast cars when a full-size version was completed in 2003. This enamel-painted casting is from the 1973 Shell promotional series.

The Demon was based on the Lil' Coffin show car and hit pegs in 1970. The casting reappeared in 1973 and was then re-released in 1993. (Tom Michael collection)

One man who recognized the cars' potential was Ken Sanger, Kmart's boys' toy buyer. In 1966, Mattel's biggest customer was the fast-growing Kmart, so convincing Sanger of the sales potential of Hot Wheels was extremely important. As such, Bernie Loomis, head of Mattel's boys' toys department, afforded Sanger a private Hot Wheels viewing before the annual Toy Fair event. An entire conference room was set aside with play sets and models, but it turns out Loomis' display was overkill.

After Sanger saw a bright-colored Hot Wheels car go head-to-head against a Matchbox car down a stretch of track, Sanger ordered 50 million of the self-selling cars on the spot. Sanger felt the number might even be too conservative. He was right.

To meet the demand for Hot Wheels cars, Mattel converted a plant in Hong Kong for the task, as well as a plant in Hawthorne, California. The goal was to produce 1 million cars per week at each plant, but it would take Mattel months to attain this target. Maintaining Mattel's quality standards, as well as the challenges in going from zero-to-die-cast cars, proved to be more of a time-consuming proposition than had been anticipated. Initially, manual labor was required to assemble the cars. Today, collectors can spot signs of this process in the chassis of some of the hand-riveted cars in which extra holes have been drilled in the bases.

The most valuable Indy Eagle is this gold chrome version.

The 1969 Grand Prix series offered such racing gems as the Indy Eagle, and in a variety of colors. These cars came with a separate decal sheet that allowed children to place the sponsor names wherever they wanted. (Tom Michael collection)

After offering the AMC AMX-based Custom AMX in 1969, Mattel followed up with the independent manufacturer's AMX/2 show car for 1971, pictured here in purple, a favorite Hot Wheels color among children in the redline era. (Tom Michael collection)

When Sanger first saw Hot Wheels cars, he predicted that Mattel would be able to sell every car it built, and he was right. When the holiday season rolled around in late 1967, store shelves were empty and people congregated around Mattel and its warehouses in attempts to score more Hot Wheels cars through Christmas Eve.

Demand for Hot Wheels cars continued through 1968 and into the next year. By November 1968, the Hawthorne plant was up to its million-cars-a-week goal, but 1969 ended with backorders for Hot Wheels cars.

Despite the success of Hot Wheels and the toy line's accompanying play sets, Mattel faced financial challenges—mainly from outside sources—during its first years of producing the die-cast cars. Backorders at the end of 1969 were partially caused by a fire at a Mattel warehouse outside of Tijuana, Mexico. In the blaze, a full third of the Christmas shipments was consumed, never to make it to market. Lost also were raw materials used to build Hot Wheels cars.

Mattel expanded the Hot Wheels line by 1970 to include such vehicles as the Sizzlers® and others, all of which fizzled. By 1971, Mattel caught up with demand and was overstocked with the die-cast cars. It also marked the first year since Hot Wheels cars hit the market that the company posted a profit loss.

The always-popular 1932 Ford also made it to the Hot Wheels line for 1969. Hot Wheels designers chose the rare Victoria model to create its classic '32 Ford Vicky, pictured here in a relatively common red color. (Tom Michael collection)

The Hot Wheels hot rod lineup increased from one car in 1968 to three cars in 1969. Among 1969's offerings was Ford's fabulous 1936 three-window coupe, which made for a handsome Hot Wheels design. As a Hot Wheels car, the classic '36 Ford Coupe featured a rumble seat that opens and closes, likely present since the hood did not open. (Tom Michael collection)

HOT WHEELS 40 YEARS

A Hot Wheels original was the Jack "Rabbit" Special, a sporty two-seater with an open cockpit only available in white. The casting debuted in 1970, and the car was used as a promotional tool for Jack in the Box restaurants. Promotional versions carry stickers on their sides and are more valuable, and because of that value, reproduction stickers have been seen. (Tom Michael collection)

Mattel expanded its Hot Wheels line yearly, from an initial run of 16 cars in 1968 up to a total of 40 the next year. Another 35 castings were added in 1970 and the same number introduced to the line in 1971. Yet, in 1972, Mattel cut the number of introductory castings down to seven.

The increase in competition was partially to blame for the decrease in introductions. The excitement of Hot Wheels spurred Matchbox to create a new line of Superfast cars, with hopes of competing not only on the sales charts, but also with accessory play sets. Mattel's inventive nature also inspired new die-cast cars, most notably Topper

Johnny Lightning cars. These toy cars featured redline tires, deep metallic paint schemes and wild engines, but were far cruder compared to Hot Wheels models.

A loss of profit in 1971 was not deserved. Since the green light had flashed for Hot Wheels cars, measures had been taken to decrease their cost of production while maintaining the flashy colors and speed prowess. It wasn't until 1972 that such measures became apparent to the general consumer, and not solely to the most detail-oriented Hot Wheels buyer.

Pin and Employee Layoffs

The most visible changes that Mattel implemented, in 1972, were with Hot Wheels painting and packaging. In the packages of the relatively small number of new castings offered that year, Mattel eliminated the collectors' buttons that had heretofore appeared with each Hot Wheels car. Up until that point, the children who bought the cars either discarded the buttons or wore them and traded the pins amongst each other.

Since pins added nothing to the play value, and the company could save 2 cents per car by not including them, they were eliminated. To further cut its overhead, Mattel laid off more than 2,000 employees throughout all divisions of the company, including design and manufacture.

The second biggest change hit the pegs in 1973. Gone were the glowing Spectraflame paint schemes. In their place were enamel colors that, ironically, looked similar to those of the competition that Mattel had bested just six years earlier. Oddly, despite the less attractive paints, sales stopped slipping and moved upward. The year also marked the manufacture of the most collectible Hot Wheels models. Even today, the 1973 castings are among the most valuable redline cars in the eyes of collectors.

In 1974, German technology added further interest and sales of Hot Wheels cars. Until then, stickers were the only graphic enhancements to some Hot Wheels cars, such as the Olds 442, Bye-

The Hot Wheels Spectraflame Classic Nomad (right) stayed alive into the enamel and tampo era, but it received a new name in 1974—Alive '55 (left).

Among the 24 new castings added to the Hot Wheels line was the 1969 Dodge Charger. This muscle car was the poster child for Dodge's "Scat Pack" performance image, which trickled down to the Hot Wheels pegs where it was equally well received. Interest in the casting hasn't died and remains strong today.

Focal, and Snake and Mongoose models. Through a pad-printing process, more extravagant designs decorated Hot Wheels cars. Best of all, the application was flush with the car, and didn't peel or scrape off as easily.

German Wilfried Phillip developed the pad-printing process, which was initially used on watch faces under the company name Tampoprint. In 1972, Tampoprint displayed its process at the National Plastics Expo trade show in Chicago, where Mattel employee George Soulakis spotted it. Since Tampoprint could put colorful designs on objects with curves, bends and crevices, Soulakis realized it would be perfect for Mattel's toys, including Hot Wheels cars and Barbie® dolls.

Mattel plunked down a full $100,000 for the equipment necessary to purchase the Tampoprint machines. Utilizing the equipment on its products required Mattel to develop a grid system across the surfaces of Hot Wheels cars to smoothly apply the graphics, but the hard work was worth it. By 1974, thanks to tampo, the die-cast cars sported a renewed flash.

The investment in pad-printing equipment struck Mattel during a low financial point. Poor sales in 1972 and 1973 made Mattel step back and analyze the future of Hot Wheels. This time, it was Ruth Handler who saved the day, saying the line should be given another year to generate the sales figures the company had set as a goal. Her patience

was rewarded with solid sales numbers of tampo-printed Hot Wheels cars in 1974, but the company was not free from trouble.

Mattel was still recovering from an investigation by the Securities and Exchange Commission, with Ruth Handler in the middle of the scrutiny. A bailout by a future mayor of Los Angeles and other investors prevented Mattel from going under, but with it came several new faces around the company's boardroom.

The stress of the SEC investigation coupled with business demands and suggestions of the new board members left the Handlers feeling detached from the business they worked hard to build. By 1975, Ruth left the company and never looked back. Elliot followed his wife within six months. Shortly thereafter, the company's headquarters and its nearly empty parking lots were put up for sale, devastating the remaining Mattel employees.

Jim Hall's Chaparral 2G was part of the Grand Prix series of redlines, which hit shelves in 1969. Like other redlines, Grand Prix Hot Wheels cars also carried pins. (Tom Michael collection)

King Kuda hit the pegs in the Spoilers series after its appearance in the Club Kit. It's pictured here in green. (Tom Michael collection)

In 1969, several original castings from the designing mind of Ira Gilford made it to die-cast form, including Torero. It was also the first year that entirely original Hot Wheels designs were used.

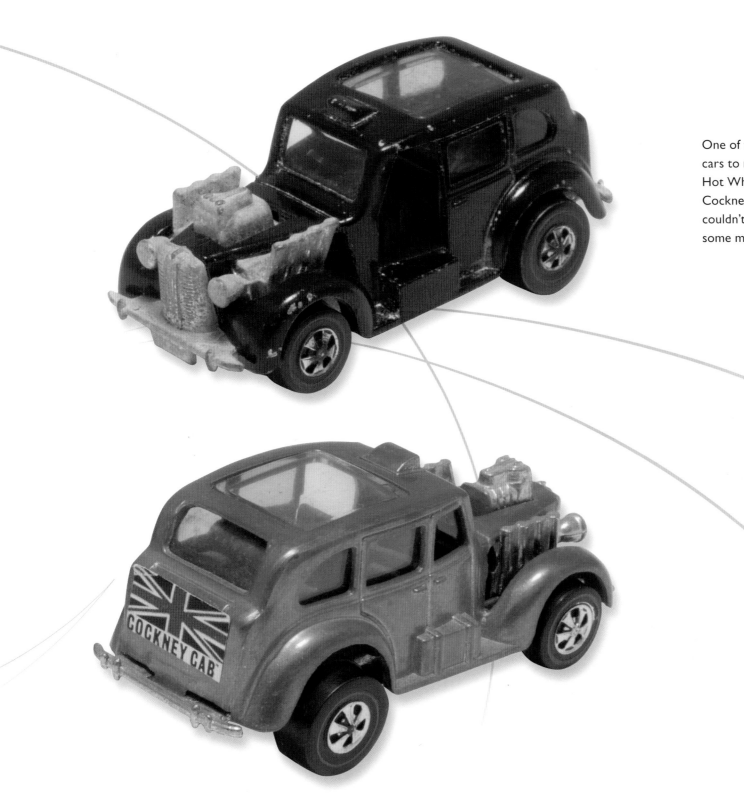

One of the few English cars to make it into the Hot Wheels lineup was the Cockney Cab. Of course, it couldn't make it in without some modifications.

Hot Wheels cars evolved quickly from the first year to the early 1970s, and one of the cars that reflects this best is the 1970s Oldsmobile Cutlass- and 442-based casting. The Olds 442 hit shelves in 1971 with the typical Spectraflame paint and sticker decorations. The casting lasted only one year, then re-emerged as Police Cruiser carrying a red light and sirens on top of its enamel white body. The door lines were removed for 1974, the base lost its cast-in engine and it gained new tampo decorations in place of the stickers. By 1976, its hood was sealed and a plastic base was used as a cost-saving measure. The Olds 442 spawned other variations, including Chief's Special, Army Staff Car and Maxi Taxi.

A rear spoiler, and an exposed and blown engine transformed the Hot Wheels original Custom Mustang casting into the chrome Boss Hoss, which was available as the first Club Kit car in 1970.

The Club Kit team from 1970: Each of these castings was available to children who joined the Hot Wheels Club. In addition to one car, each child received a club magazine, iron-on patch and Hot Wheels Club membership certificate in a Club Kit box for $1.

Several different numbers were applied to the chrome body of Boss Hoss while it was offered in the Club Kit. After its tour of duty in the Club Kit, Boss Hoss was available in the aptly named Spoilers series in 1971, represented here by the red example.

Also modified for the Club Kit was Custom Camaro. After it lost its opening hood and gained more punch with a bigger engine and a rear deck spoiler, the casting earned a new name: Heavy Chevy. This casting followed the Boss Hoss as the 1970 Club Kit car.

A combination of the design skill of Howard Rees and Harry Bradley in 1970 resulted in the Sky Show Fleetside, a casting that added more play value to the Custom Fleetside from 1968. The truck was part of the Sky Show or Flying Circus set and included three planes in blue, green and yellow.

For 1970, Mattel introduced a series of wild, futuristic trucks from the designing mind of Ira Gilford called Heavyweights. The cab of each Heavyweights vehicle was strikingly similar, thus providing consistency to the line.

Mattel kept a stock of clever people on its staff, including a group that came up with names for toys. Employees in this group were called "name smiths," and among them was Carol Robinson, who came up with catchy names for all of the Spoilers, including TNT-Bird.

Available from the 1970 Club Kit was the King Kuda, which was a modified casting based on the Custom Barracuda. This one has lost its stripes and number to time, which allows the chrome body to shine without distraction.

Designer Larry Wood is said to have a soft spot for classic cars (those recognized by the Classic Car Club of America), and the Classic Cord is a product of that affection. Of course, the car received the Hot Wheels touch with Lakes-style pipes and an engine that poked through the hood.

Spoilers are increasing in value, and it's about time. Most of the castings in the Spoilers line were based on already-existing Hot Wheels "Custom" counterparts, but with more new hot rod-style tweaks. Among those Spoilers to debut in 1970 was Light My Firebird, which had a counterpart in 1969's Custom Firebird.

Even more hopped-up Hot Wheels cars debuted for 1970 in a new Spoilers series, which took existing castings and ripped off their hoods to make room for a bigger engine and dumped on front and rear spoilers, stickers and stripes. Nitty Gritty Kitty was one of those wild new castings; its roots were in the Custom Cougar.

At one dollar a pop, kids could gather quite a number of Hot Wheels cars, and Mattel was prepared. The company offered a variety of cases that not only carried Hot Wheels cars, the compartments within the cases also helped keep cars in fine condition.

Mighty Maverick was only in stores from 1970-'71 before it was replaced by Street Snorter, a more tame version of Ford's Maverick and without the Mighty Maverick's wild spoiler. The spoiler on the pictured blue example is intact, while the black plastic spoiler on the pink Mighty Maverick shows how the spoiler can break over time.

When Mattel bought Monogram Models, it also received rights to the model company's designs. Among them was Tom Daniel's Red Baron, which Mattel offered throughout the 1970s, but only in red. The version here hails from the model's inaugural year of 1970. (Tom Michael collection)

To create Bye-Focal for 1971 and '72, Hot Wheels designers filleted and stretched a Dodge Challenger's proportions to create an entirely new car. Because of a low quality of metal used to build some Bye-Focal chassis, many bases have developed tiny cracks and have become known as "crumblers."

Salvation to Mattel's Hot Wheels 1974 line came in the form of tampo decoration, which brought back some of the glimmer of the Spectraflame era. Heavy Chevy was brought back for 1974 wearing the new tampo, and it wore them well. Two colors were offered: the enamel yellow pictured here, and a more rare, light-green version.

A 1956 Ford F-100 formed the basis of this wildly customized 1971 casting, Short Order. By pulling out the orange, plastic tailgate, the bed on the truck can be expanded.

Long popular with collectors is the Olds 442, a 1971 casting that Larry Wood scaled down from full-size car proportions to Hot Wheels size. The casting is based on a 1970 Oldsmobile 4-4-2 Holiday Coupe and features a removable plastic spoiler. Mattel applied stickers to some castings at the factory or left it to each car's owner to apply them (or a combination of both). For the Olds 442, a sticker sheet with star-emblazoned stripes was left in the bottom of the blister pack and not every Olds 442 owner applied them. Today, that sticker sheet, if complete, has become quite valuable.

Cars from the short-lived
Spoilers series continue to
grow in popularity, and one of
those castings with a large fan
base is Sugar Caddy, a casting
designed by Ira Gilford.

Which way is it going? To
create T-4-2, Larry Wood
took two Ford Model T front
ends and mounted them
back-to-back. Each end is
identical with an exposed
engine and front bumper.
Because the original name
of this car was "Which
Way?" Larry Wood placed a
question mark on each door.

Times were tough at Mattel in the early 1970s, and cost-cutting measures were taken in 1973 to lower the expense at which Hot Wheels cars were built. For 1973, the Sand Crab from 1970 was stripped of its clear roof and Spectraflame paint and renamed Dune Daddy for 1973. In place of Spectraflame paint, Dune Daddy received enamel paint.

Although the flash of Spectraflame paint is gone, as is its clear roof, Dune Daddy hails from a year in which Hot Wheels cars are particularly valuable. The enamel cars are highly sought because of their rarity, and because many were only offered in 1973.

The staged rivalry between Don "Snake" Prudhomme and Tom "Mongoose" McEwen was reduced to Hot Wheels scale when the company began sponsoring the Plymouth Barracuda and Duster funny cars pictured here, as well as the rail dragsters, driven by McEwen and Prudhomme. The funny cars have popped into the Hot Wheels lineup, either on cards or in play sets, several times throughout the years.

In 1971, Tom "Mongoose" McEwen's Plymouth Duster was issued a second time, this year in blue or light blue. Represented here is a light-blue version showing off its infrastructure, which included an engine and seat, as well as props to hold the metal body up. When in a blister pack, only the stickers on the passenger side were applied by the factory, as it was the side visible in the pack.

HOT WHEELS 40 YEARS

The only vehicle from the Heavyweights series that didn't receive the futuristic Ira Gilford styling was Tom Daniel's S'Cool Bus. Daniel worked at Monogram, which was purchased by Mattel, and his model of S'Cool Bus was downsized and cast in metal for the 1971 Hot Wheels line. The Chevy-based bus was chopped and featured a twin pair of engines, presumably of 427 cubic inch displacement, hence the "854 C.I.D." stickers on its hood.

Because Road King Truck was only offered in the Mountain Mining set, which itself was only offered in 1974, this casting is one of the rarest vehicles to emerge in the Hot Wheels line. And, it was only offered in enamel yellow.

Pad-printed tampo added an attractive design element to Hot Wheels cars, a fact that didn't get by children. Thanks to these decorative features, Hot Wheels sales rebounded. Tampo returned for 1975 and graced the body of Gremlin Grinder, shown here in its first release (at top), as a rare Herfy's restaurant promo (at bottom) and as a Super Chrome model from 1976 (center).

A sleeper among Hot Wheels collectors is Custom Continental, pictured here in one of its most desirable colors, light blue. The fine specimen shows toning or mottling, a trait common to Spectraflame Hot Wheels cars as the zamac (zinc, aluminum, magnesium and copper) metal body beneath corrodes unevenly.

The strong following for Volkswagens in the Hot Wheels line stems from this casting, the side-loading Beach Bomb, pictured here in blue, and its far more rare, rear-loading counterpart.

Don't let the pretty background and desirability of the Olds 442 casting blind your wallet. The paint condition of this car, and the prevalence of magenta appearing on the Olds 442 casting, make this an entry-level version of this casting in the $100-200 range. If it were wearing pink or purple, it would be worth a lot more

Colors Matter

All colors aren't equal, at least in the world of redline Hot Wheels collecting. And, even when a desirable car in an equally desirable color does surface, the overall condition of the car and its paint play an extremely important part in the car's value to a collector.

The advent of the Internet auction trading pool has added a fresh level of convenience in searching for rare, vintage cars, as well as selling them. This also allowed collectors to become even pickier when it came to finding cars to add to their collections, so determining values and condition has become more important than ever. That, presumably, is why you are holding this book in your hands.

Ironically, it seems big boys and girls prefer their Hot Wheels cars in pink, unusual for a toy considered so masculine. Plus, they typically have no problem paying for it, often doling out money that would buy several examples of the same casting in the same condition. Why? The feminine color was obviously not very popular with boys when the cars were new, and many long-time collectors believe few Hot Wheels cars were painted pink.

You can bet this Classic Cord is worth more than its original price tag states. The color is called light green, but many collectors refer to it as apple green. In this color, the extremely popular casting, based on the Gordon Buehrig-designed 1937 Cord 812 Phaeton, is worth more than $200 in mint, loose condition. If it were pink, it would fetch more than $1,000.

Light blue looks great on the Classic '57 T-Bird, and while many other castings are relatively rare in this color, the level of rarity on this casting is only moderate. (Tom Michael collection)

Of course, most castings have a color that will attract a premium, but it tends to vary; what is common in one casting may be rare for a different casting. For instance, the price of a magenta Evil Weevil is one of the casting's highest, but an Olds in the same color fetches the casting's lowest value.

Now, before you pull out your wallet and lay down a small fortune for that pink redline Olds, an understanding of grading the Spectraflame paint's condition is critical. Time can be devastating to

the highly metallic, sometimes almost chrome-like paint surface of the early redline Hot Wheels cars, and that's just the start.

The presence and condition of decals on cars that should have them also affect the cars' values. Even the manner in which these decals (crooked or even incorrectly) have been applied to the cars weighs heavily on the cars' values. It is not out of the question to find very nice cars with values that are 70 to 80 percent that of mint-condition loose examples.

Bye-Focal models carry two prices. The magenta version of this beloved casting is valued at approximately $150, while the light-blue model is worth more than $500. In dark blue, the value drops to the $200 range.

Time punishes Hot Wheels paint with chipping, flecking and toning, but only chipping can be credited to the love and play of children. The latter two can be found on cars that have never even left their packages in the past 35 years or less.

Toning, characterized by dark splotches, affects nearly every color applied to the Hot Wheels castings, regardless of whether the cars left their packages. The same is true for what flaw collectors refer to as "flecking," or pin-size chips that flake off the Spectraflame-painted cars. Hot Wheels cars suffering these flaws, even to a small degree, find themselves with cars worth half the value of mint-in-package examples, sometimes less.

Missing paint, especially in severe circumstances, is definitely the most value-affecting flaw; expect to pay only 10 to 30 percent of the mint price when a car is missing 50 percent or more of its paint. These cars also tend to have other flaws to their bases, wheels and glass, which must also account for the low pricing.

It's not unusual for pink to be the most valuable color a casting can wear, and that's the case when it comes to the Custom AMX from 1969. This two-seat AMX product can be found in salmon pink and hot pink, which is pictured here.

A defect that seems to be isolated to one color, at least in my experience, is corrosion to light blue Olds 442 castings. When this happens, the paint does the opposite of toning and the car's finish can develop white splotches. These cancerous spots are like leprosy to collectors who typically fear the damage cannot be reversed. On average, the values of such cars are about 20 to 30 percent the value of mint examples in the same color.

Because value is so dependent on redline cars' conditions, and so many flaws can develop through time, some collectors take matters into their own hands and restore cars back to new condition. While there definitely is room for these enthusi-

One of the most coveted colors of Hot Wheels cars from the start was purple, and many collectors today recall their childhood days spent hunting for any casting in purple. Today, purple remains popular, but a car's value depends on how common the color is found on that casting. In Classic Nomad's case, the color isn't necessarily rare, putting the car's value at the middle of the pack.

asts in the collecting field, especially the talented artisans, the cars are not nearly as valuable as non-restored examples in mint or even lesser condition, so beware for collectors trying to pass off restored cars as counterfeits. Look for clues of disassembly, such as flaws, poor alignment and tampered rivets, and you will be able to get what you pay for.

As with any large purchase, research is the key to a pleasant transaction. Use these tips to know what to look for and make your redline purchase an intelligent one that your pocketbook won't regret.

Light green on redlines is rapidly increasing in popularity, particularly on muscle car castings. Look for cars like this light green or "apple green" Custom Charger from 1969 to become more valuable in the future. (Tom Michael collection)

Orange may be a relatively common color on Turbofire, but there's a reason—it looks great. The dark splotches in the paint are common in all redline-era colors, and collectors call this discoloration "toning" or "mottling." It is caused by moisture in the metal body, and it affects the value of a Hot Wheels car. (Tom Michael collection)

Most Hot Wheels cars were issued in several colors, but Paddy Wagon was one of only a few to be offered in only one color—dark blue. This casting was offered several different times through the years. This example hails from 1970, its inaugural year. (Tom Michael collection)

Custom Firebirds with matching interiors are particularly sought, and this rare combination is mostly seen on red and blue. There are a few brown-on-brown Custom Firebirds, and since the color itself is not commonly found on any Custom Firebird, this example is particularly desirable.

Chapter Three

WHEELING THROUGH THE '70S, AND BEYOND

More Mopar muscle cars began hitting the pegs after the turn of the century, and among them was the '71 Plymouth GTX, pictured here as a 2001 First Editions model.

Anew era in die-cast cars sprouted from the low points Mattel endured in the 1970s. In the Hot Wheels line, attention was paid to the cars' earliest and most important features—their wheels.

Realizing that Hot Wheels cars were intended to remind children of their older brothers' cars, and that redline wheels had fallen off the option list of U.S.-built vehicles several years earlier, Mattel eliminated redlines from the wheels on all of its cars.

The change occurred midway through 1977, leaving the year's castings available with two types of wheels: redlines and "blackwalls." The measure also saved the company a considerable amount of money in production costs and helped Mattel regain a profitable status.

Aiding the company's recovery was a new method of marketing Hot Wheels cars by placing them in categories or series. It helped that these series proved to be popular, and they also left children and collectors feeling inclined to purchase them all. Super Chromes, Scene Machines, Flying Colors and other series featured a variety of castings with matching decorations and packaging to make them easy to pick out in a sea of Hot Wheels cars.

In 1976, the ever-popular Deuce roadster joined the Hot Wheels line. The car, Street Rodder, came from Larry Wood's pen, and is little changed from his original artwork for it. Many children found enjoyment plucking and replacing the chrome plastic engine from its bay.

Along with the Letter Getter-based The Incredible Hulks Scene Machine, a more futuristic The Incredible Hulk van was also released in 1979 as part of the Heroes series. To add further confusion, two versions with varying rear windows were built.

Mattel also teamed up with Marvel Comics to create the Heroes series that counted on the cross-over appeal of toys and comic book characters to sell Hot Wheels cars. "The Thing," "The Incredible Hulk," "Spider-Man" and other comic book celebrities all made special appearances in the Heroes series, much to the children's delight.

Before long, Mattel was back underneath its Hot Wheels cars for some tuning to the cars' chassis. The company went into its engineering archives to revive an old idea that had never been implemented—a chassis that could be jacked up like a high schooler's air-shock-equipped Chevelle.

The idea dated back to at least the mid 1970s, when prototypes based on a '57 Chevy and Rodger Dodger chassis were constructed, but the adjustable wheels didn't hit shelves until 1980. The new chassis debuted on such new classic-car castings as the 3-Window '34 and '40s Woodie.

To make the rear ends of the cars point to the sky, a chunk was taken out of the chassis to make way for a gray plastic piece that held the rear axle and wheels. The plastic piece could be clicked to several different positions that would raise and lower the car to a child's preferred height, thus adding to the play value on which Hot Wheels cars had been founded.

Continued attention was paid to the chassis in 1981, when "Hot Ones" hit the shelves. The new cars featured six-slot gold wheels mounted on free-rolling 1960s-style axles and earned Mattel the right to tout it had the "fastest non-powered die-cast metal cars" once again. The company wasn't afraid to boast its accomplishment and capped each blister card off with a sticker identifying its gold-wheeled cars as Hot Ones until a new blister card hit stores.

Laying Rubber

Only two years later, Mattel took one step back in speed technology but two steps forward in design when it revealed new "Real Riders" wheels and tires on select cars. While the rubber didn't afford Hot Wheels cars the speed its plastic-wheeled cars had been known for, Real Riders brought a realistic look to its cars. Real Riders were rubber tires sporting the "Goodyear" name on turbine-style wheels like those seen on the 1969 Dodge Charger in the popular TV series "Dukes of Hazzard."

The wheels gave Mattel a choice of outfitting cars with knobby 4x4 tires or street car tires, depending on the casting, but almost as importantly, children could take the tires off and on at their whim.

Originally, Mattel planned on making the wheels of Real Riders gold, but to keep the price under $1, they were molded in gray or white. Though the wheel hub and tire designs have changed since they debuted in 1983, Hot Wheels cars with Real Riders tires remain a favorite and can still be found on current collector-series castings.

The introduction of Real Riders tires sent a new energy to the pegs, but their success wasn't enough to keep Mattel in the black. For the second time in 12 years, the company faced bankruptcy. The financial woes could not be attributed to Hot Wheels or Barbie, but Mattel's other non-toy holdings. To recover, the company concentrated on the toys it was so successful delivering.

For 1983 and that year only, Mattel offered the Hong Kong-built '40s Ford 2-Door. In that short time, the casting was offered with black walls and Real Riders tires with white or gray wheels. The casting reappeared little changed in 1985 as the Malaysia-built Fat Fendered '40, and it's been popular ever since.

Larry Wood did what every car collector dreams of doing—immortalizing his own car in scale. This '32 Ford Delivery was inspired by Wood's own fat-fender Ford sedan delivery. This casting was first offered in 1989, and it's represented by this yellow example. The casting is very popular with collectors and has appeared in several colors since.

Mattel also required an influx of cash as its stock values foundered and its net worth fell into negative figures—$136 million in the hole, to be exact. Financial recovery came from John L. Vogelstein, a director of Mattel. He brought $231 million to Mattel's coffers, which allowed the company to proceed with what it did best, build toys.

Tough times weren't over yet, however. Big layoffs hit the toy company in 1985. To further reduce overhead costs, the company moved production of some Hot Wheels cars from France and Mexico to Malaysia. Another series of layoffs struck in 1989, and other employees saw themselves moved to different departments.

Despite decreasing staffing levels and other changes, a super hero landed behind a desk inside Mattel's executive row in 1988. He didn't wear a cape or tights, but new Mattel CEO John Amerman knew that there was untapped potential in the Hot Wheels and Barbie brands, and set out to capture more of the toy market with Mattel's bread-and butter toys.

Amerman helped launch collector's editions in both toy lines, made licensing agreements with successful brands like the animated TV show "The Simpsons," and cemented product tie-ins with McDonald's and its Happy Meals. Amerman realized the potential Hot Wheels cars had in Western Europe, where die-cast cars are popular.

New marketing methods in the Hot Wheels line created series of cars with common tampo patterns or other features in the 1970s. For the 1979 Scene Machines, that meant allowing children to peer into the back window of a Hot Wheels car to see an image of "The Incredible Hulk." This casting was based on 1977's Letter Getter, but it was renamed "The Incredible Hulk" for the series.

Mattel's appreciation for the classics showed through again in 1977 with the '31 Doozie, a casting based on a Derham Tourster-bodied Model J Duesenberg, last known to be owned by author Clive Cussler. '31 Doozies built early in 1977 received redlines; cars built later in the year received black walls, and are less valuable than the redline counterparts.

Retooled for Toys R Us

Street rods were hot through the 1970s and into the early 1980s, and no one knew that better than the street rod man, Larry Wood. This 3-Window '34 hit in 1980 as one of the Hi-Rakers models, a system that allowed the rear wheels to be raised and lowered to increase the toy's play value. This version from 1984 also benefits from Mattel's Real Riders wheels, which put removable rubber tires on the corner of Hot Wheels cars in the series. Today, castings sporting these tires are far more valuable than black wall versions.

Through the 1990s, Mattel tapped its history and its retail outlets, as well as other well-known brands, to disseminate Hot Wheels cars, and collectors ate up everything that debuted. A special anniversary series available only in Toys R Us stores recreated eight redline-era Hot Wheels cars from 1968-'70 and showed up on pegs in 1993. The retooled Hot Wheels models proved successful and were continued into 1994.

Collectors were driven to toy stores and toy de-partments in record numbers when Mattel sprung a surprise for 1995. The company had done its homework when it came to what adult collectors were looking for, and that year the company released several new series that would reinvigorate the toy hobby.

Hottest among the debuts was a 12-car Treasure Hunt series. Treasure Hunt cars came in limited editions of 10,000 each and featured the popular Real Riders tires. To build anticipation for

Treasure Hunts, Mattel spaced out its release to one car per month. The series alone increased the public's awareness of Hot Wheels cars being not only extremely collectible, but also valuable. The series created many new Hot Wheels collectors and mom-and-pop Hot Wheels businesses that sell the toys on the secondary market.

Stimulated interest in Hot Wheels cars, timed with highly popular new models in 1996, such as the Customized VW Drag Bus and 1970 Dodge Daytona Charger, sent Hot Wheels cars steam-rolling into rekindled success. More great new castings followed, and the number of new castings each year began to increase from around a dozen each year to 40 or more new cars per year.

Collector desires were further fueled in 1996 by a new line of Hot Wheels cars sold individually or in sets under the name "Hot Wheels Collectibles." The fresh models were extremely detailed with price tags to match their expensive construction,

One of the biggest castings to ever swing from the pegs was the GMC Motor Home, which struck stores in 1977. To create the vehicle, Larry Wood had to scale down and re-proportion a full-size drawing of the motor home given to Hot Wheels designers by General Motors. The gold GMC Motor Home here is the most valuable, usually trading on rare occasions for more than $1,000; it was a Mattel promotional toy from 1978.

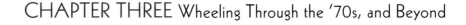

Just like the Volkswagen Rabbit that it was based on, the well-traveled Hare Splitter was available across the globe. The white version, complete with a tire rack, was manufactured in Hong Kong, Malaysia and France with minor light and dark tampo variations and base differences, while the same model without tampo and an orange tire rack was a French casting; the yellow version was available in India.

and many were based on famous hot rods and customs of the day.

A wild 1949 Cadillac-based custom built for ZZ Top's Billy Gibbons and the famous Barris brothers-built Hirohata Merc are just a couple examples that sparked the line, which rapidly expanded to include a giant catalog of castings.

Unlike the "basic" series of Hot Wheels cars that sell for around $1 each, Hot Wheels Collectibles feature tiny, separate parts for bumpers and grilles, a choice of trim and often wheels created exclusively for the car to maintain their realism. Hot Wheels Collectibles also adhere to a consistent 1:64 scale

more frequently than their slightly smaller basic series counterparts.

Building on its success, Mattel asserted its popularity over longtime competitor, Matchbox, by purchasing its parent company in 1997, exactly 30 years after Hot Wheels cars rolled onto the market. By the time of its sale, Matchbox was several owners removed from its original England-based parent company, Lesney Products. Mattel had passed on the opportunity to purchase Matchbox on at least two previous occasions, but when Tyco Toys and all of its holdings, which included Matchbox, were offered in the late 1990s, Mattel added the compa-

Using a similar chrome finish introduced on the 1970 Club Kit cars, Mattel included a Super Chromes series in its line beginning in 1976. The series continued through 1977 and included the Poison Pinto in the series that year. The chrome casting appeared only in the Super Chromes six-pack, but with redlines or black walls.

The opening hood returned to Hot Wheels cars in the 1979 Hare Splitter, a Volkswagen Rabbit-based casting. During the earlier redline era, nearly every lift-up hood was cast in metal. By the 1970s, Hare Splitter was one of the few castings with an opening hood; it was now a plastic part.

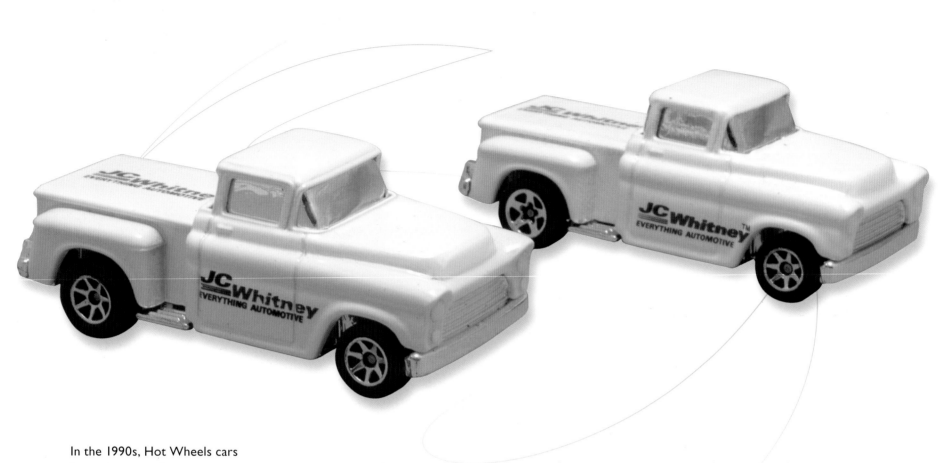

In the 1990s, Hot Wheels cars began being used to promote companies and their products more frequently. Due to their limited runs, they also became popular collectibles with Hot Wheels collectors. These '56 Flashsider models are prototypes for the five-hole versions that were offered in the 20,000-car run. Note the seven-spoke wheels on the promotional vehicle in the foreground; the final version released sported five-spoke wheels.

ny's subdivisions (and their accompanying toys) to the Mattel portfolio.

Many feared the consolidation of Hot Wheels and Matchbox under one parent company would be the end of Matchbox cars, but just the opposite happened. Today, Mattel separates the two divisions by continuing the Matchbox tradition of offering realistic cars in its line, and focuses its Hot Wheels line on hot rods and fantasy vehicles.

An avalanche of great castings and revitalized interest in Hot Wheels cars, especially by adults who remember trading them at school recess during the redline era, created a swell of promotional Hot Wheels models to be offered in 1999.

Mattel built no less than 60 promotional premiums for such companies as Lexmark, JC Whitney, Jiffy Lube and even large automotive events and publications. Generally, the cars were produced in limited numbers, from several thousand to tens of thousands, and were priced at a premium. Many of the cars featured high-end packaging and top-of-the-line Real Riders, and were available only through the company that commissioned them or the secondary market. Mattel had figured out how to hook the bait, and collectors began biting—hard!

For its 25th anniversary, Mattel reissued eight castings from the first three years of Hot Wheels production. The cars were packaged in original-style blister cards and were close enough to the originals, the car has to be flipped to note the "Hot Wheels Vintage" embossed in the base. This metallic ruby red gem replicated the '32 Ford Vicky. (Jackie Aschittino collection)

One of the world's most valuable cars is the teardrop-shaped Figoni et Falaschi Talbot-Lago, and one of the most valuable Hot Wheels cars from the 1990s is the blue and black Talbot Lago from 1999, shown here. These cars fetch nearly $400 in mint condition.

WATCH THE HOT WHEELS CAR RACE ON TV!

HOT WHEELS... LEADING THE WAY!™

DIE CAST METAL & PLASTIC PARTS. FOR AGES OVER 3 YEARS.

Hot Wheels

MATTEL ®

GUARANTEED Hot Wheels ® FOR LIFE

TALBOT LAGO

COLLECTOR #714

1930s STYLESETTER!

17965

Mattel even priced Real Riders models, including this Street Rodder from 1982, at the same price point as their black wall counterparts.

One of 1977's longest-running and most-popular castings is the '57 Chevy. At first, the casting was available only with a covered engine, but several years after it hit pegs, the '57 Chevy gained a metal engine rising from the hood.

Beginning in 1981, Mattel dressed some of its castings with new gold Hot Ones, wheels which spun around 1960s-style axles and allowed Mattel to claim its cars were the fastest non-powered die-cast cars. In 1982, the wheels were mounted on the 1980 Chevrolet Malibu-based Taxi, making the car one fast people hauler.

R6447>
P643>9646"

EMBROIDERED PATCH OFFER. SEE BACK!

Hot Wheels

DRAG STRIPPERS

Hot Wheels
MATTEL

DRAG STRIPPERS

DIE-CAST METAL!

30 Show Hoss II
No. 9646

Snake and Mongoose were gone by 1977, but Mattel hadn't forgotten about funny cars. At the close of the 1970s, Show Hoss II joined the Hot Wheels lineup as a member of the Drag Strippers.

Snake and Mongoose were on hiatus, but the Firebird Funny Car filled in the flip-top duties in the Hot Wheels line starting in 1982.

Hot Wheels designer Larry Wood's affection for classic cars showed itself again with the 1934 Packard Super Eight- or Twelve-based sedan. This majestic casting was only offered in black during its 1983 release and its 1997 re-release. Wood also included a slightly modified version of this casting in the Larry Wood World Tour set, which commemorated his 35 years at Mattel. It, and a subsequent sELECTIONs version, featured colors other than black and came with blanked-out quarter windows. This is one of the author's favorite childhood castings.

Classic cars began reappearing in the Hot Wheels line in the early 1980s and among them was the Mercedes 540K. The casting was built in Hong Kong and Malaysia; this black version with whitewalls was built in Malaysia with black walls or whitewalls in 1988.

"Masters of the Universe," a Mattel toy series dating to the 1980s, and the Hot Wheels Cadillac Seville met to create this France-only casting.

Caught in the crossover: When American Tipper debuted in 1976, it wore redlines like all other Hot Wheels cars before it and like those offered the same year. But early in 1977, all Hot Wheels cars, including American Tipper, were stripped of the red stripe as a cost-saving measure. American Tipper's face was a familiar one, as the headlight and grille ensemble was similar to 1974's Road King Truck, but the castings were otherwise very different.

Among the most popular castings with Hot Wheels collectors is the '55 Chevy from 1982. The casting wore 26 different decorations and several variations of these since it was first offered. The '55 Chevy was retired in 2001, when it joined the Final Run series. It's shown here as a youthful casting and as it appeared when first released.

It was like the clock turned back. In 1968, the Hot Wheels Custom Corvette beat Chevrolet's full-size version to market. In 1983, this '80s Corvette hit the market, even though the new, full-size version wasn't available until the 1984 model year because Chevrolet didn't sell Corvettes in 1983.

Another pop culture tie-in in the Hot Wheels line was this 1984 version of Baja Breaker, which received a black paint job with red stripe. For this version, Baja Breaker looked similar to the van used in the hit TV series "A Team."

An old favorite returned in 1983—the Custom Camaro, which was renamed and slightly modified to be the '67 Camaro. Initially, the '67 Camaro was used somewhat sparingly, and coupled with the popularity of the model, early versions like these are coveted. The red '67 Camaro with flame tampo was the first release of the casting, while the metallic lime version was available only in a 15th anniversary belt buckle three-pack.

Hot Wheels models were intended to replicate cars children would recognize, and a lot of their parents drove Dodge Aries station wagons. This interesting casting of such a ho-hum car was only offered in the United States in 1982 and in Mexico two years later with a different color interior and a lighter brown wood grain tampo.

Volkswagens have always been popular and somewhat prevalent in the Hot Wheels line, so the Sunagon from 1982 is a natural fit. The casting features a metal body and chassis with a removable plastic top. The orange version was offered in United States, but the red model is an international edition.

Building on its successful history with funny cars, Mattel re-entered racing with Pepsi Challenger in 1982. This casting was similar to 1978's Army Funny Car, the next year's Human Torch and Screamin' from 1985.

In the early 1980s, Mattel added a white stripe to some of its wheels, and none wore them better than the classic cars in the Hot Wheels lineup. One of those classy castings was the '31 Doozie, shown here as a rare Malaysia-built casting with red plastic fenders and interior against a red body.

The '65 Mustang Convertible is one of the rare castings from the mid 1980s with an enduring popularity today. In 1998, this blue version hit pegs.

This squad car has been around the block and working in a variety of security-based professions. In 1983, the casting was in airport security guise. Here, the relatively rare Airport Security wears blue paint for the European market. However, the Masters of the Universe edition with *"Le Club de Maitres de L'Univers"* on the hood is the more valuable version of Airport Security.

In 1984, Mattel offered these shimmering 1980s muscle cars for one cent and two proofs of purchase for each car. Today, the Camaro Z-28 is slightly more valuable than the '80s Firebird, and each sells for around $20.

Also new in the early 1980s were Camaros and Firebirds, and Mattel cast the former one year after its 1982 model year introduction. For 1983, the '80s Firebird exploded onto the market. The pictured versions date to 1992 and show the three rare color, wheel and tampo variations.

Conversion vans were big in the 1970s and into the 1980s, and Dream Van caught the tail end of the fad. The casting featured an opening door on the driver's side, and all United States versions featured Real Riders tires. The green version with black walls was only available to the India toy-buying market.

Carroll Shelby's Classic Cobra is on a long list of popular Hot Wheels castings, but these early blue versions, dating from the mid 1980s, are among the most coveted. The yellow-striped version is a Mexico-only casting valued at more than $100 in mint condition.

Despite its awkward proportions and unrealistic design, many versions of Gulch Stepper are relatively valuable to Hot Wheels collectors. The black version (both shown here are black) is one of the more collectible versions; the version at top is worth approximately $10, while the version at bottom sports a reversal of colors in the tampo, making it worth five times as much.

Mattel introduced a series of cars that changed colors under the name Color Racers. Three-car sets in the Color Racers series changed colors depending on whether hot or cold water was poured on them. This '55 Chevy was offered in the series in 1987 and is shown midway through the color-changing process.

At the tail end of the redline era, a 1956 Ford F-100-based truck casting appeared. After a short run, the casting disappeared, and then reappeared in 1985 as the Good Ol' Pick-Um-Up. In this version, the truck sported a new color, Real Riders tires and lost its truck bed topper.

Full-size Talbot-Lago teardrop coupes are so valuable, they are the candy of the super rich. Mattel's version was far more affordable at the $1 Basic car price, and values for the first versions, which were available in burgundy or white in 1988, have only risen 10-fold, at most.

A throwback to the redline era was the VW Bug, a casting similar to the Custom Volkswagen from 1968, though the modern version featured a sealed hood as its most noticeable difference. This casting hit pegs in 1989.

Many children who grew up in the 1990s remember the Peterbilt Dump Truck, especially in red since there were many minor variations, and it was available with several different wheels. The difference between the two versions here is relatively minor, but the truck in the foreground has rare white wheels with dull centers, making it worth more than $50 in mint condition. Meanwhile, the version in the background is far more common and worth about a tenth of the rare Peterbilt.

Mattel matched up two competing semis to create the Great American Truck Race set. In it, Peterbilt and Kenworth tractors left their cargo behind and became Hammer Down (Peterbilt) and Movin' On (Kenworth). As tractors only, these castings appeared solely in the series and so they are relatively difficult to find.

Custom Mercs have always been popular in scale form, but none has been as well received as Larry Wood's Purple Passion from 1990. The casting sent surges of collectors to the pegs and price rises well above the $1 retail price. Despite its name, the casting does not wear the purple color in every release. The version with green scallops represents the initial release of the casting; the flamed version is a 1993 version.

Compounding the resurgence in popularity of Hot Wheels cars in the mid 1990s was the release of the VW Bus in 1996. This casting is the Hot Wheels heavyweight champion as the line's heaviest casting, and since its initial offering, it's always been offered with collector value in mind. This version was offered with an Official Collector's Guide CD-ROM in 1999.

Street rods have made popular Hot Wheels cars, and so Mattel keeps offering them on the pegs. Tail Dragger is based on a '41 Ford coupe and looks as though it's just rolled out of Sam and George Barris's California shop.

Another street rod to hit the Hot Wheels lineup was the T-Bucket, represented here by the first version of the car from 1989.

A new level of detail struck the Hot Wheels line with the debut of Hot Wheels Collectibles in 1996. Tiny plastic chrome pieces, accurate wheels-and-tires and other details were usually found only on larger-scale replica cars. The detail carried a price. The four-car Barris Customs series was offered to the hobby with a $120 price tag, but the price quickly spiraled downward as collectors showed reservations about the price. Pictured are the Barris Brothers' famous creations of, clockwise from bottom left, the two-tone green Hirohata Merc, Ala Kart, Elvis Dream Cadillac and the 1949 Mercury. Nearly every car in the Hot Wheels Collectibles line strictly adhered to 1:64 scale, unlike basic cars.

Mattel slipped a new series on to the pegs in 1995, and it caused a new buzz among collectors and introduced new people to the hobby of collecting Hot Wheels cars. The Treasure Hunt series featured cars with a very limited run and fit them with desirable Real Riders wheels and tires. This '59 Caddy hails from the 1996 Treasure Hunt series of 12 cars.

For scale car-carrying duties, Mattel issued Ramp Truck, a Kenworth-based toy truck that has been popular with children because it could carry many other Hot Wheels cars on its back. The casting debuted in the Crack-Ups line with a grille that could be smashed in, then spun back around to look new. A version with a fixed grille of the Kenworth-based truck appeared in 1991 and was retired in 2001 in the Final Run series. This version hails from 1992.

Not all castings in the 100% Hot Wheels line were in sets priced at more than $100. Without compromising the quality, Mattel also offered two- and three-car sets priced at $20 and $30, respectively. One of those sets included this princely pair of classics— a supercharged J. Gurney Nutting Duesenberg Model J built for the Maharajah of Holkar and a Van Vooren-bodied Bugatti Type 57 commissioned by the French government for the Shah of Persia on the occasion of his wedding. Hot Wheels designer Larry Wood was in charge of scaling down these currently California-based cars for the Classic Bodies 100% Hot Wheels line.

Hot Wheels collectors love the company's '67 GTO, and even more so when it features Real Riders wheels, as it does here as part of the Auto Affinity series.

Many Hot Wheels models in the 1990s wore Hot Wheels Race Team livery, which consisted of blue paint and a large Hot Wheels flame logo on the side. Among the cars to wear the Hot Wheels Race Team graphics was the Olds 442 W-30.

One of the many three-car sets in the Hot Wheels Collectibles line was this set of Cadillacs decorated for the Hard Rock Café franchise. The set included a 1959 Cadillac convertible, chopped 1964 Cadillac coupe (which Mattel mislabeled as a 1963 model) and a 1959 Cadillac Seville.

Among the many promotional Hot Wheels cars commissioned by companies in limited numbers was this '55 Chevy, which was built to promote *Old Cars Weekly News & Marketplace* in 1999. Many of these cars came individually packaged in small boxes with windows. The box for the car looked like the rear end of a 1955 Chevrolet Bel Air. The 1990s saw a huge surge in such promotional Hot Wheels offerings.

Of all the different paint schemes applied to the 1959 Cadillac Eldorado Seville in the 100% Hot Wheels line, the prettiest to be applied to the car was this shade of pink.

This '57 Cadillac Eldorado, based on an Eldorado Seville built by famous finned Cadillac customizer John D'Agostino, appeared in the Signature '57s Legends set in 1997. Like all Hot Wheels Collectibles in the Legends series, the set this car was a part of carried a steep, $100-plus price tag.

Plymouth's lightweight Savoy model was modeled for the 100% Hot Wheels line. This '63 Plymouth was decked out like one of drag racer Dick Landy's Plymouths from the 1960s.

A much more wild street machine to hit the pegs is the Hot Wheels Surf Crate. This casting plays on the growing popularity of wood-bodied street rods.

Early in the life of the 100% Hot Wheels line, this 1957 Oldsmobile Golden Rocket 88 coupe was offered in Petty family livery. The 1:64 car was true to the car Richard Petty drove in the 1950s.

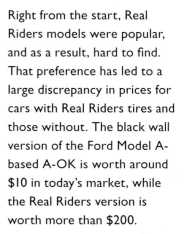

Right from the start, Real Riders models were popular, and as a result, hard to find. That preference has led to a large discrepancy in prices for cars with Real Riders tires and those without. The black wall version of the Ford Model A-based A-OK is worth around $10 in today's market, while the Real Riders version is worth more than $200.

Only 700 of Cadillac's ultra-luxurious Eldorado Brougham were built from 1957-'58, but Mattel built many more as collectors ate them up when the casting debuted in 2002.

V-aluable W-heels

Beetle-sized Hot Wheels Volkswagens fetch busloads of bucks

When choosing which vehicles to offer, Hot Wheels designers select popular cars that will catch the eye of cool-car-hungry children. But even for them, the dedicated following for Volkswagen-based castings is surely shocking.

The first VW-based design to come out of Mattel did so drenched in Spectraflame paint during the die-cast car's inaugural year of 1968. That Hot Wheels model was the Custom Volkswagen, and the Beetle featured an engine poking out of the wrong end—the front.

Most of the cars also featured clear sunroofs that could be slid open in the spirit of play value, but some models surfaced in Europe with solid roofs and no sunroofs. Values for the sunroof-sporting versions of the Custom Volkswagen are in line with other castings from the original "Sweet Sixteen." For those few Custom Volkswagens with the sealed and solid tops, the value is "over the roof" and creeps into the $1,000 range for mint examples.

Better be careful—this isn't a $15,000 rear-loading Beach Bomb, it's a recently made car built by Bright Vision, and it is reportedly based on an original side-loading Beach Bomb. When these became available at a Hot Wheels convention, many well-known collectors traded $500 and a side-loading Beach Bomb to own one of these well-done castings.

The following year, Mattel followed up with the Microbus-based Volkswagen Beach Bomb, which isn't surprising since the toy company was based in Southern California. The area was a hot bed of hot rods, custom cars and even economical-yet-trendy Volkswagen models. Surfing was also a popular activity in '60s So Cal, and Hot Wheels designers paired up the popular hobbies when it designed the Beach Bomb for 1969.

The first Beach Bombs featured surfboards poking out the back windows and sunroofs in the center third of the tops. After a relatively small number of the castings were manufactured in Hong Kong, Mattel's quality manager noticed the vehicles were top-heavy and tipped easily on stretches of orange track. Mattel managers also noticed that the castings, which came to be known as rear-loading Beach Bombs, with their slim sides, wouldn't go through the Hot Wheels Super Chargers.

Since play value was and is an important element of the Hot Wheels philosophy, designers went back to their sketchpads and reconfigured the VW Beach Bomb to be wider and less top heavy. The result was a pod flanking each side of the car, which doubled as a surfboard carrier, and an enlarged sunroof that ran the entire length of the Beach Bomb body.

The base was also given added heft to keep the wheels planted towards earth and to further overcome the obstacles that kept it from performing as well as other Hot Wheels cars. The new version became known as a side-loading Beach Bomb, and was produced in far greater quantities.

Despite their relatively common nature, mint side-loading Beach Bombs fetch healthy prices in the several-hundred-dollar range. Because of their desirability, even rough versions of the casting approach the $100 mark.

Here are the production versions of the Beach Bomb, which feature the side-loading surfboards used to make the Volkswagen fit through the Super Chargers and lower the car's center of gravity to keep it on slices of orange track.

Beach Bombs in the Pink

Side-loading Beach Bomb values pale in comparison to those of the rear-loading Beach Bomb, however. In fact, no other Hot Wheels casting even comes close to comparing to those of the rear-loading Beach Bombs, which carry prices that start in the five-figure range and extend up to the $70,000-plus price paid, in 2000, for a Spectraflame pink version. (The seller was said to have bought a Dodge Viper with the money, as in a full-size Viper!)

So desirable are the rear-loading Beach Bombs

that in 2001, Bright Vision, a Murietta, California-based company, was selling reproduction rear-loading Beach Bombs for $500. The cars debuted at the Hot Wheels Collector Nationals in Oak Brook, Ill., and many well-known collectors lined up to purchase examples of their very own, which were extremely close to the originals.

Because Bright Vision stated its rear-loaders were actually based on side-loading Beach Bombs, it also required purchasers to trade one of the more

Nothing says "Flower Power" like a Volkswagen bus decked out with flower stickers. Just like the full-size Volkswagens, the Beach Bomb from 1969 was often found with such decorations during the Vietnam war era.

common side-loaders as part of the deal. The company sold out of its 40 customized rear-loading Beach Bombs in 10 hours.

Mattel quickly followed up with its own version of the rear-loading Beach Bombs, but changed the casting enough to safely separate it from the rare originals, of which approximately 25 are believed to still exist. The casting, dubbed Beach Bomb Too, debuted during the 2002 holiday season on the Hot Wheels Collector site in runs limited to 10,000 cars in each of three Spectraflame colors: purple, red and green.

The first Beach Bomb Too models featured rear-loading surfboards and looked like a toy car taken right out of the redline era, but it also sported blacked-out side panels, rather than the open side windows on the originals.

The premium-built cars regularly fetch more than their original $15 price and now command $25 or more, but collectors seek out the special pink version, of which only 275 were made for Mattel employees during the 2002 holiday season. Hot Wheels fans often pay several hundred dollars for recent pink Beach Bomb Too models, which is more than some vintage side-loading Beach Bombs from the redline era fetch.

The Volkswagen tradition continued into the 1980s with the Sunagon, a VW Vanagon-based casting first offered in 1982.

After the run was completed, the company destroyed the rear-loading Beach Bomb Too tooling and began offering side-loading versions, which are still available in special runs at its web site. The sale of these cars smacks of history and illustrates the car's full circle path. A truck version followed in late 2006.

Other Hot Wheels VW models popular with collectors include the VW Bug, Baja Bug and Volkswagen New Beetle Cup, but none comes close to the popularity of the VW Bus (a.k.a. Customized VW Drag Bus). When this casting hit store pegs in 1996, it hit them hard.

With a metal body that flips up from a metal base, the casting became the heaviest Hot Wheels model yet. Its popularity with collectors has never wavered, and its flat sides make it the perfect billboard—a premium offering used by several companies as a promotional tool. "First Edition" models can fetch $10, with the original retail price tag being a dollar, and other versions are valued at $100 or more, which is unheard of from other modern castings. Mattel followed this model with a truck version, the Customized VW Drag Truck, in 2005.

Custom Volkswagens were produced in the United States and Hong Kong. This Custom Volkswagen was produced in Hong Kong—the headlights cast as part of the chassis and poking through the fenders is the give-away. (Tom Michael collection)

The Custom Volkswagen from 1968 was long gone when this VW Bug casting debuted in 1989. Collectors welcomed the car, and realizing its popularity, Mattel began cranking out several versions of the casting. This black version with Real Riders tires was offered to SEMA Show attendees in 1993.

Since the beginning of Hot Wheels cars, Volkswagens have been spotted in the lineup. Here is a sprinkling of Custom Volkswagens from the inaugural year of 1968.

Shown is a group of highly
sought VW Buses. Only
the blue version from 1996
was available on the pegs.

Combine the most popular series of Hot Wheels (Treasure Hunts) with the most popular casting (VW Bus) and you have an extremely desirable collectible. Each year, 12 Treasure Hunts are created, but to honor the tenth anniversary of the series in 2005, this 13th Treasure Hunt was built.

In 1996, Mattel debuted a casting that would immediately form an unofficial fan club, the VW Bus. After its initial appearance in the 1996 First Editions series, the casting, Mattel's heaviest Hot Wheels car, was reserved for special sets and limited edition status.

Nine—count 'em—nine rear-loading Beach Bombs stand tall among other prototypes owned by Michael Strauss and displayed at the 2005 Hot Wheels Collectors Nationals in Chicago.

Since there are so few rear-loading Beach Bombs, the Hot Wheels Collectors club staff had this rear-loading version built in 2002. The run was limited to 10,000 in each of three colors, and 275 in pink for employees, making its production run of 30,275 the least amount of one casting built in Hot Wheels history. After the short production run, the casting and its mold were retired.

Larry Wood creates a run of only a few hundred holiday cars for Mattel employees, but for the Red Line Club, the master himself designed this side-loading Beach Bomb Too for club members in 2003.

Through Hot Wheels history, three different castings bore the name Evil Weevil: the Volkswagen Beetle-based 1971 version, a scorpion-looking casting from 1986 spelled slightly differently (Eevil Weevil) and this revived version for the Hot Wheels Collectors club in 2005. Pictured is a pre-production sample.

Unlike its VW Bus brother, the VW Drag Truck was available more than once on the pegs. The casting was available at retail outlets in the vintage-style Hot Wheels Classics series.

The final Neo-Classics model from the 2006 Hot Wheels Collectors Club was the new Beach Bomb Pickup, offered in December of that year in Spectraflame pink with pink flames and redlines.

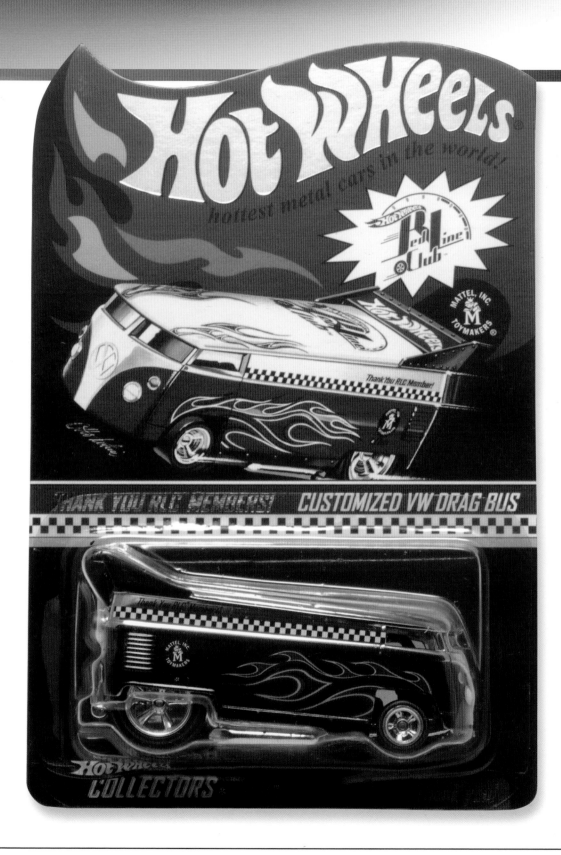

Nothing says "thank you" like a free instant collectible, and the Red Line Club did just that for its members in 2005 with this redline-equipped version of the VW Bus.

Chapter Four

LOOKING BACK TO MOVE AHEAD

A Hot Wheels original, Qombee, debuted in 2006. Volkswagen influences can be seen in the car's nose.

Mattel opened its doors to collectors, almost literally, in 2001 with the introduction of the website HotWheelsCollectors.com. Never before had collectors been able to get an inside view of Mattel's inner workings, or communicate directly with the people responsible for creating Hot Wheels cars. All that changed through the website forums, which continue to be moderated by Hot Wheels staff members.

In 2002, Mattel expanded the site to include the Red Line Club, which models itself after the Hot Wheels club of 1970 and its exclusive chrome-plated muscle cars. The modern Red Line Club is responsible for bringing back realistic red line wheels and some of the most rare castings from the early days of Hot Wheels cars.

On the Red Line Club and Hot Wheels Collectors forums, club members can voice their opinions as to which cars should be built, some-

To celebrate the 35th anniversary of Hot Wheels in 2003, a new Hot Wheels Highway 35 series of cars hit stores with co-molded wheels and fusion graphics. To lead off the series, a special Toy Fair Deora II was decked out in Hot Wheels Highway 35 fusion graphics.

For the Hot Wheels cars Collectors Club, recent favorites were retooled to make them fit in with castings from the early days of Hot Wheels cars. This 1970 Chevelle was made part of the Neo-Classics line in the Hot Wheels Collectors Club and received redlines on a metal base, as well as a new opening hood.

Mattel brought back 1970 with this 1970 Chevelle in the Hot Wheels Collectors Club Neo-Classics line. The casting debuted in 1999, but in 2005, a metal base returned and it was given an opening hood.

times down to color and wheels choices, sharing their opinion in "sELECTIONs" voting. From their home computers, club members vote in waves on which of four vehicles will be cast, in what color, tampo design and, eventually, wheels selection. It's like ordering a new car from a catalog, but on a much smaller scale (and budget).

For the 35th anniversary in 2003, Mattel revolutionized some of its cars with new wheels and a fresh way of dressing them up. The changes were first implemented on the Hot Wheels Highway 35 series, an anniversary line that included many popular castings incorporating the company's new co-molded wheels. The new "shoes" for Hot Wheels cars followed the trend in full-size and scale-model cars of sporting large-diameter wheels wrapped with thin tires.

Mattel also debuted slick fusion graphics on the Hot Wheels Highway 35 series, which allowed for clear, intricate designs on its cars. Tampo, the

signature dressing of Hot Wheels cars since 1974, was phased out later in the year within other lines in favor of the fusion graphics.

Collectors were also able to witness an evolution of Hot Wheels cars in 2003. Cartoon-like castings with exaggerated engines and body features, including severely chopped tops and out-of-proportion fenders, hit the pegs in the 2003 First Editions series. Muscle car-based castings with the exaggerated design elements fared well with collectors, but they left other types of models in the series on the pegs for children to scoop up.

The following year, Hot Wheels designer Larry Wood celebrated a 35th anniversary of his own, and to mark his three and a half decades with Mattel, he hit the road, traveling across the United States and overseas to Japan. Along the way, he gave out specially decorated 'Tooned Shift Kicker castings, a hot rod-based casting he had recently designed.

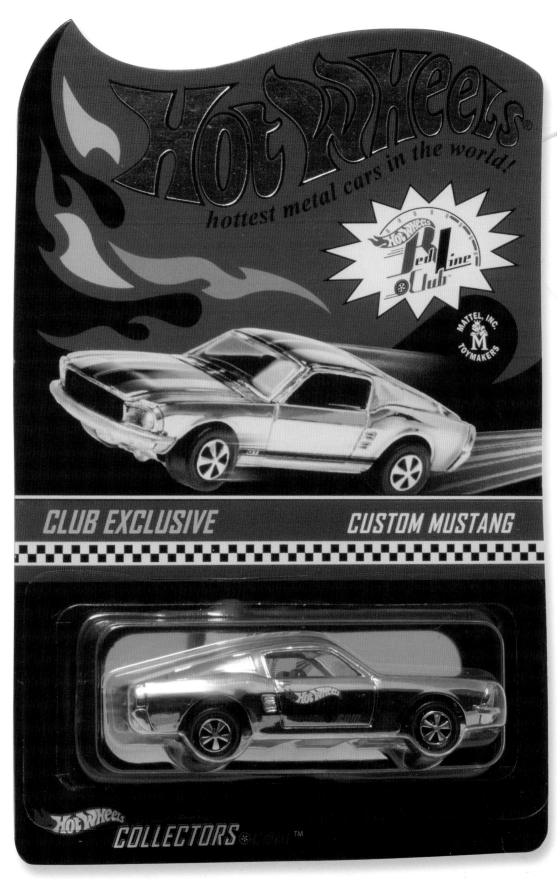

In 2002, the Custom Mustang was awarded Red Line Club duty, and it wore the customary chrome body plating. Ironically, the original Custom Mustang casting was modified to produce the Boss Hoss for the first Hot Wheels Club in 1970.

Cadillac's prototype Sixteen concept car was first captured as a realistic rendition of the hardtop sedan by Mattel, but the toy maker followed up in 2004 with this out-of-proportion version in 2004 in its Hardnoze category. The casting went by the name Hardnoze Cadillac V-16 Concept.

Dizzying Editions

The party at Mattel was just getting started. Building on the 35th-anniversary momentum, the company offered an unprecedented and dizzying 101 new castings in the 2004 basic car line. Initially, Mattel set out to offer 100 new Hot Wheels cars for what it called the "Hot 100," but a mid-year addition of a special new VW Drag Truck upped the ante one more casting.

All Volkswagen-based cars earn their Hot Wheels name, and this VW was no different. To create the entirely new casting, Mattel based its proportions on the already hot VW Bus from 1996, but gave it a truck bed rather than a van body. To add the casting to their collections, Hot Wheels

fans had to swing by their local Toys R Us store and buy 20 cars in one visit, mail in the UPC codes and complete an order form. The postman delivered the car several weeks later.

Some collectors cringed when more of the exaggerated castings joined the 2004 First Editions series. The cartoon-like-designed cars earned their own series names and were broken up into categories such as Hardnoze, Fatbax and 'Tooned, which continued to cater to Mattel's largest customer base—children.

A line of realistic models was also offered, but the cartoon-like Hardnoze and Fatbax cars began to grow on adult collectors, and even inspired other

The Red Line Club not only brought back club cars decked out in a chrome finish, just as they had been in 1970, it brought back old castings from the redline era. This Olds 442 is one of those revived castings in its chrome 2005 club car configuration.

In 2005, the second-generation Olds 442 did club duty. Red-, blue-, black- and white-striped versions were available; this black-striped version is one of 6,000.

An insane number of new cars hit the pegs—100, to be exact—in 2004. The last of 2004's "Hot 100" to strike the pegs was Cool-One, an original casting sporting a lot of 1970s van culture, mated with ice cream fantasies. A special release of a Customized VW Drag Truck available in a mail-in offer put the total number of 2004 First Editions castings to 101.

It was 1968 all over again when Hot Wheels Classics hit the pegs for 2005. The cars featured Spectraflame paint, all-metal construction and 1960s-style Hot Wheels packaging.

die-cast car manufacturers to build models with similarly exaggerated bodies and large wheels as the "dub" fad caught on.

While its basic line headed for the future, a special Hot Wheels Classics line was created to look back on Mattel's past. For 2005, a series of Spectraflame-coated castings with metal bases were discreetly debuted at the 2004 Specialty Equipment and Market Association Show in Las Vegas.

Three retro-packaged and styled castings were sandwiched into a small corner of a glass case: a green '67 Dodge Charger with doors and hood that open; a '67 Mustang fastback; and a pink Passion. Following the show, associate marketing manager and former HotWheelsCollectors.com website moderator Ray Adler (HW Ray) provided details

about the recently built vintage-style castings with an old-school Hot Wheels look.

"Essentially, this line brings everything that is great about Hot Wheels over the last 36 years into a collectible line at retail. We are featuring 25 of the best Hot Wheels ever made, consisting of muscle cars, hot rods and the best original designs together in one retro-themed line," he said.

For further vintage appeal, Hot Wheels designer Otto Kuhni, who designed the package artwork on the first Hot Wheels cars, was employed to bring the current Purple Passion casting back to 1968 for the blister pack art. The cars hit store pegs in the first quarter of 2005, and were as difficult to obtain as the first Hot Wheels cars in 1968. Eventually, the line inspired new castings initially exclusive to Hot Wheels Classics.

When the Red Line Club started in 2002, it offered the '67 Camaro as the membership car as a throw-back to the 1970 club, when a Camaro-based Heavy Chevy was included as one of the three Club Kit cars.

The Super Chromes series kept popping up on the Hot Wheels radar, first on the pegs in 1976, then again in 2003 as online exclusives, and back to the pegs in 2003. This 1957 Chevy Bel Air hails from the 2003 series.

Faster Than Ever Wheels Peel Out

At the end of the 2005 season, Mattel revealed Faster Than Ever wheels in its basic Hot Wheels series. These wheels looked strikingly similar to the co-molded wheels introduced on the Hot Wheels Highway 35 series two years earlier, and they claimed to live up to their name.

During this crossover period in which the wheels went in to use, many 2005 basic cars, including new designs, could be found with the traditional five-spoke wheels or new Faster Than Ever wheels. Collectors climbed store pegs in search of all of each casting's wheel variations.

Before the introduction of Hot Wheels Classics, the popular retro-styled Hot Wheels cars could only be found online at HotWheelsCollectors.com. Following the success of Hot Wheels Classics, more old-time Hot Wheels models became available in retail outlets. But instead of going back to the 1960s, Mattel went back to the 1970s and offered new Super Chromes and Flying Customs cars, all of which sported vintage graphics and packaging.

Alongside the series, Mattel added a new Lowriders line that sported 1970s-looking graphics and packaging, despite the fact that the series had

Castings with wild proportions and unusual names joined the 2004 First Editions series. This casting appeared in the Fat-bax series and carried the name "Exhausted," both of which it earned.

Batmobiles surged into the Hot Wheels line in the 2000s, and by 2004 Mattel was even offering its own takes on the "Caped Crusaders'" rides. This Batmobile was from the 2004 Crooze series.

Sizzlers cars returned to store shelves, but only those at Target, in 2006. The play sets and cars and even packaging were right out of the 1960s.

never been offered before. The new series struck Target store toy aisles in fall of 2006. Additionally, the 1970s' short-lived Sizzlers cars were revived and offered exclusively at Target stores that year.

Eight Sizzlers cars started swinging next to Super Chromes and Flying Customs cars that fall, and nearby, a vinyl carrying case, Giant "O" Race Set, Mad Scatter Set and Juice Machine could also be picked up. Several adults likely found themselves wearing pajamas while playing with their new Hot Wheels cars and watching Saturday morning cartoons again.

The idea of creating Sizzlers cars was first pitched by Mattel employees in September of 2005. But before Target was approached to sell the line exclusively, the Hot Wheels staff hit the books.

Through research, Mattel's John Ludwig and other staffers determined which Sizzlers products would return to store shelves.

"I can't tell you how many times I've had someone say to me, 'Please bring back Sizzlers' when they find out I work on Hot Wheels," Ludwig said upon the Sizzlers cars' reintroduction. "The idea of bringing back Sizzlers has been floating around Mattel for years now. It was a team effort that was hatched in part by the folks who work with Target, and that is why the line is a Target exclusive. Target wanted something truly special, and when we pitched Sizzlers, they jumped all over it."

To maintain the appealing history behind Sizzlers cars, Mattel used vintage Sizzler toys to create the new versions.

"We made models from the original items," Ludwig added, "which was great because we had a physical reference for each item. The goal we set for ourselves in bringing back Sizzlers was to be as true to the originals as possible. We started with original Sizzlers vehicles, track and accessories, and we worked directly from those original items to create the new versions. If you look at the vehicles, for example, we tried to do everything like the originals that we could, right down to the markings on the chassis and bodies."

To make Sizzlers cars safer some improvements were made along the way without harming the play value or vintage look of the cars or sets.

Keeping Hot Wheels products viable also requires looking to the future, and while Mattel kept an eye on the rearview mirror with its past, it looked through the windshield at partnerships that would benefit the Hot Wheels name.

One of those cooperative efforts put Hot Wheels cars back into cereal boxes. The collaborative effort between Mattel and Ford Motor Co. resulted in pocket-sized Hot Wheels Ford Fusions being offered in Kellogg's cereals. The move helped Ford create buzz around its new full-size Fusion, and pointed collectors to the food aisle of Target stores, because the new casting couldn't be found swinging on pegs in a toy aisle.

A similar promotional method of casting a new car exclusively for one market had been used earlier to introduce the new 2002 Saturn Ion Quad Coupe at the New York Auto Show.

The Mighty Maverick returned to the long list of Hot Wheels offerings in 2005, but it was only available through HotWheelsCollectors.com in the club's Neo-Classics series. The pictured example is a pre-production sample.

The first revived Olds 442 to become available was the Real Riders version, available only to Red Line Club members as it sold out before becoming available to HotWheelsCollectors.com members in 2004.

Motorcycles were far and few between in the Hot Wheels line, but they came back in a big way with the Scorchin' Scooter. The vehicle has appeared more than two dozen times since it first hit pegs in 1997.

Beginning in 2004, Mattel began breaking up its new models into categories. Airy 8 came out of the 2005 Realistix series, which included vehicles that looked roadworthy, but weren't necessarily vehicles that were produced by manufacturers. This 2005 First Editions Airy 8 is a purple variation.

Once Scorchin' Scooter was well received, motorcycles came barreling to the pegs. Blast Lane followed in 2002 and was as popular as Scorchin' Scooter, but hasn't appeared nearly as often.

Not all new castings were wild at the start of the 2000s. This Alfa Romeo B.A.T. prototype from the 2005 First Editions series may have looked like a Hot Wheels original, yet it was actually based on the Bertone-bodied Prototipo Alfa Romeo B.A.T. 9 from 1955.

A view into the soul of Hot Wheels cars was available in the 2005 First Editions series X-Raycers. Ten of them were offered, including this new casting, Stockar.

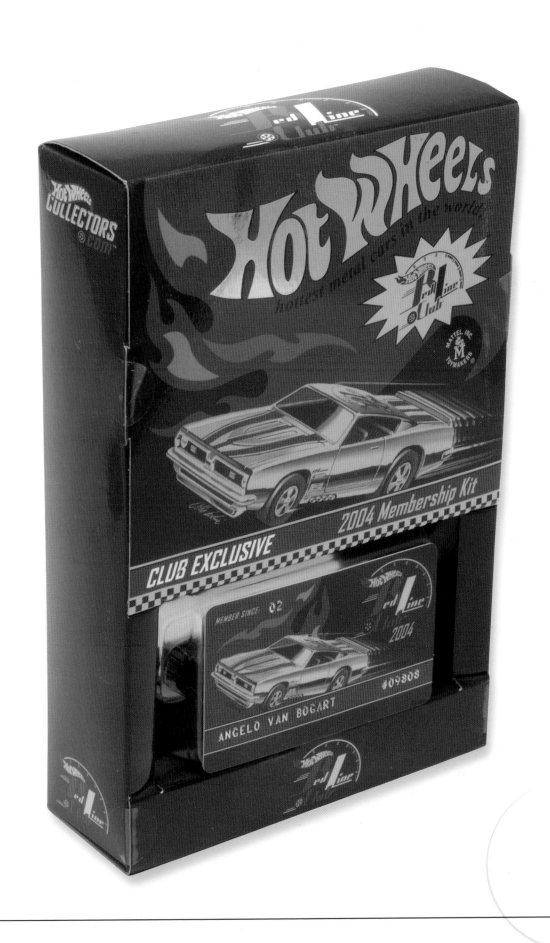

For the 2004 Red Line Club, the customized Barracuda casting was brought back, right down to the chrome covering its body. Hot Wheels dubbed the car Custom Cuda this go-round, and, as it did every year, changed the color of the club car's stripes.

Which car a member received depended on how soon he or she renewed. The first 5,000 cars received red stripes, the next 7,000 cars received blue stripes and the final 8,000 cars were dressed with black stripes. Of course, the red-stripe versions are most coveted for their rarity.

Mattel offered a short-lived line of cars in the Auto Affinity series that had more detail than basic cars. Among those cars offered was the Dodge Dart, which was based on a 1968 model.

Collectors clamor to the pegs for the Hot Wheels '67 GTO, and this period drag car-looking version from 2001 is among the more popular, but common, versions.

The Plymouth Barracuda funny car raced by Don "Snake" Prudhomme slammed in and out of the Hot Wheels lineup numerous times since 1970 as Snake and Plymouth Barracuda. In recent times, the casting has gone by Plymouth Barracuda, although it's not much different from the 1970 and subsequent versions. This version sporting Real Riders tires was built for the Hot Wheels Club of Japan Official Fan Club in 2002.

Manufacturers didn't always create their prototype vehicles, but Mattel was making a habit of offering them in the early 2000s. For 2005, Hot Wheels added the Ford Bronco Concept to its Blings category. As a part of the Blings series, the Ford Bronco Concept sported unusually large wheels.

Hot Wheels Collectors Club members can interact with Mattel staff members, and one of those ways is voting on castings and what colors, design and wheels each will wear. This blue Classic Packard is the result of voting in 2004. This casting differed from the original Classic Packard casting first offered in 1983 by having a blanked-out quarter window.

Among the lines of Hot Wheels castings with exaggerated features in 2004 was the Crooze series. This classic car-based Ozzenberg, with a stretched-out tail, was among those Crooze cars.

Mattel bilaterally sliced and diced full-size cars to create the Torpedoes series. In 2005, a bullet-nose Studebaker coupe was shaved for the Torpedoes series.

Hot Wheels cars were squashed like bugs on a sidewalk for the Drop Tops series of 2005 First Editions models. This casting went by the name "Flattery," an appropriate name for such a ground-scraping casting.

You've heard of the Visible Man, but here's the visible '69 Chevelle, courtesy of the 2005 First Editions line, which included a category of see-through cars in the year's X-Raycers series.

In 2003, a bit of the cocktail cruiser movement from the late 1950s and early 1960s hit the Hot Wheels line with the Pontiac Bonneville 1965.

After years of being ignored by all manufacturers in scale, Mattel released a casting of the 1962 Chevrolet. This '62 Chevrolet, representative of the '62 Bel Air "bubble top," was released in the Auto Affinity line.

HOT WHEELS 40 YEARS

Cadillac wowed crowds by reviving its V-16 engine in 2003, but it took Mattel to bring the car it was in, the Sixteen, to reality in 2004.

After years of being the black sheep of the "Big Three," popularity among muscle car Mopars was really heating up when Mattel offered this '66 Dodge Charger among its 2000 First Editions models.

Mattel encourages adding more play value to the Hot Wheels line, and one way that can be done is making the body removable, as it is on the Hot Wheels Mini Cooper.

After 33 years, the Classic Cord returned to the Hot Wheels lineup, courtesy of the Hot Wheels Collectors Club. To protect the sanctity of the original Classic Cord from 1971 and 1972, a few minor changes to the car's proportions and the manner in which the window fit the removable top were undertaken when the car debuted in 2005.

There was already a Dodge Challenger in the 100% Hot Wheels line, but this 2006 First Editions '70 Dodge Challenger in the basic line brought the car to within a child's allowance.

The Red Line Club offered its new releases to Red Line Club members first, and it paid to be a member. Many cars sold out before they were available to the general public, like the side-loading Beach Bomb Too from the 2003 Super Chromes series.

Among the most famous Hot Wheels cars is the ultra-rare rear-loading Beach Bomb. Since only a literal handful survive, Hot Wheels Collectors Club replicated the original in 2002. The most obvious change from the original rear-loading Beach Bomb was the blocked-out side windows on the new Beach Bomb Too.

Hot Wheels Treasure Hunts

Take one of the most popular castings and throw in the first year in a popular series, and you have the most coveted Treasure Hunt of all, the '67 Camaro from 1995.

Digging for treasure became a lot more fun in 1995. That year, Mattel released 12 special "Treasure Hunt" models to retail markets and spurred a boom in Hot Wheels collecting. Up until that time, collectors searching for rare variations had to be savvy when it came to picking out scarce and valuable cars, usually doing so by hunting down paint and wheel variations.

To accomplish the feat, a collector needed a mind like a steel trap to remember which versions were more common and a keen eye to notice such derivations.

Production of Treasure Hunts was capped to 10,000 of each casting in the first years they were available. It was also the first time Mattel offered limited-edition castings on the pegs, and for only

$1 apiece! Membership in the elite Treasure Hunt series was advertised and touted on each blister pack via a green band across the card spelling out that the car inside was special among the $1 "basic" cars around it.

Thanks to the Treasure Hunt packaging, special paint schemes and each model's high-end wheels, the hot collectible nature of Treasure Hunts didn't get past many Hot Wheels enthusiasts, or even beyond the people who stock the toys on store shelves. The value of the castings inspired store employees to set Treasure Hunt cars aside for themselves.

Some collectors even paid the store employees to hide the cars when stocking Hot Wheels cars, saving them for the collector to find later. Stories of clerks hiding the cars in bath towels, among girl's toys and even under bottom shelves in the toy departments are not uncommon.

Collectors with fewer contacts in retail stores were known to wait in their cars or outside store doors until they opened. To get the best pickings, other collectors timed the employee schedules and showed up as cases of Hot Wheels cars were being placed on the pegs.

Such shenanigans frustrated Mattel and its retail outlets, but there was, and still is (as Treasure Hunts are still made), little it could do about the

'59 Caddy Treasure Hunt from 1996.

problem. The toy manufacturer devised other ways of making the cars more difficult to spot for unscrupulous "peg vultures" and speculators who sought to profit from the cars.

The financial appeal to speculators remains. Once a new Treasure Hunt hits store pegs, its value escalates far beyond the $1 price. It's not uncommon for a new Treasure Hunt to fetch a price in the $50 range, especially if it's an already-prized casting, such as a muscle car or vintage vehicle.

Mattel schedules the release of all of its castings throughout the year (usually one per month), and once a subsequent Treasure Hunt lands on store pegs, the high values realized by the previous model fizzle and the next Treasure Hunt release stirs excitement. However, at several times their original sticker prices, values for all Treasure Hunts remain much stronger than their basic model counterparts.

Retail giant J.C. Penney began offering complete sets of Hot Wheels Treasure Hunts at premi-

From the beginning, Treasure Hunts were offered in complete sets around the holidays each year through catalog retail giant J.C. Penney. Just like the individual cars they hold, these sets are very valuable.

um prices, and timed the sets to hit shelves around the holidays each year. Packaging the cars as a set made collecting Treasure Hunts a one-stop opportunity, but it took the fun out of searching for the rarities throughout the year. Regardless, it is one way a collector can corral a set, and the annual offerings remain popular.

As with most toys, the first or earliest models tend to bring the most money, and Treasure Hunts are certainly not exempt from this trend. In 1995,

Mattel built 10,000 of each Treasure Hunt model in the series, which consisted of the '67 Camaro; '31 Doozie; Classic Cobra; Classic Nomad; Purple Passion; Olds 442 W-30; Stutz Blackhawk; '35 Classic Caddy; Rolls-Royce Phantom II; Corvette Split Window; VW Bug; and '57 T-Bird. Of these, the '67 Camaro remains the most popular, and valuable. This already popular muscle car casting regularly fetches around $300 for a mint-in-pack example.

So Fine Treasure Hunt from 2001.

Mighty Sums for Rare Variations

Variations are among the most sought-after Hot Wheels cars, and such casting derivations have not escaped the Treasure Hunt series. Although only 12 Treasure Hunts are typically released throughout each year, variations in wheels, colors, tampo and other features create more opportunities to collect Treasure Hunts. Hot Wheels fans latch onto such chances, and often pay mighty sums to acquire the most rare variations for their collections.

In honor of the 10th anniversary of the highly successful Treasure Hunt series, Mattel picked one of the most popular castings from each year and integrated it into the 2005 line. Such castings as the '67 Camaro, '67 Pontiac GTO and '70 Plymouth Barracuda again hit the stores with special Treasure Hunt hardware, such as high-end wheels and special paint jobs for another round of T-Hunt duty.

The company also did something it had never done before in the Treasure Hunt series—it offered a 13th car, and didn't make it available on store pegs. For the special occasion, the company introduced the downright famous VW Bus to the series.

Getting the casting required dedication from the collector. By purchasing 20 basic cars during each of the year's four quarters, and obtaining a coupon verifying the purchase of the 20 cars within the promotional period, a collector could mail away for the special 13th Treasure Hunt. Collectors also received a bonus car during each of the four periods, and, in turn, each of those became collectible.

In another twist, random "winners" receive the VW Bus early during each promotional period. For all of the effort it takes to obtain them, the VW Buses are among the most collectible and valuable modern Treasure Hunts.

Due to the popularity of Treasure Hunts, Mattel has produced more each year to meet demand, though it still caps the number to maintain collector interest and the aura surrounding the special cars. The numbers of Treasure Hunts currently produced is a secret as closely guarded as security codes to enter Fort Knox, and it hasn't hurt the thrill of the hunt one ounce.

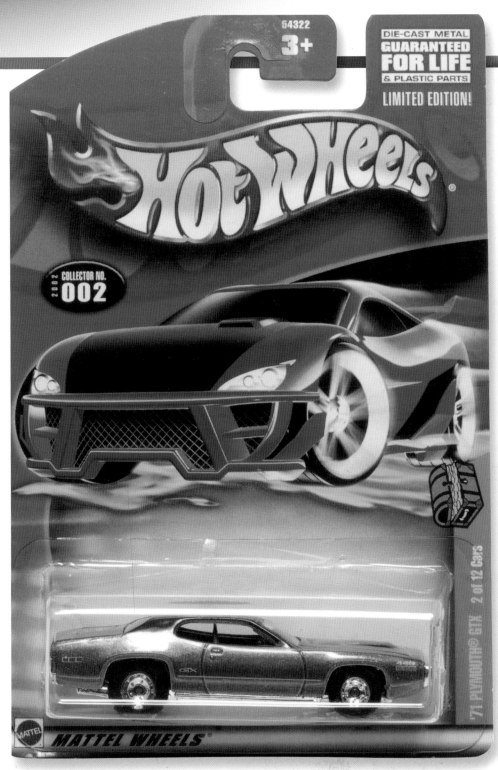

'71 Plymouth GTX Treasure Hunt from 2000.

To celebrate the tenth anniversary of the 12-car Treasure Hunt series, a thirteenth Treasure Hunt was added and it was based on the popular VW Bus for 2005.

Tail Dragger Treasure Hunt from 2002.

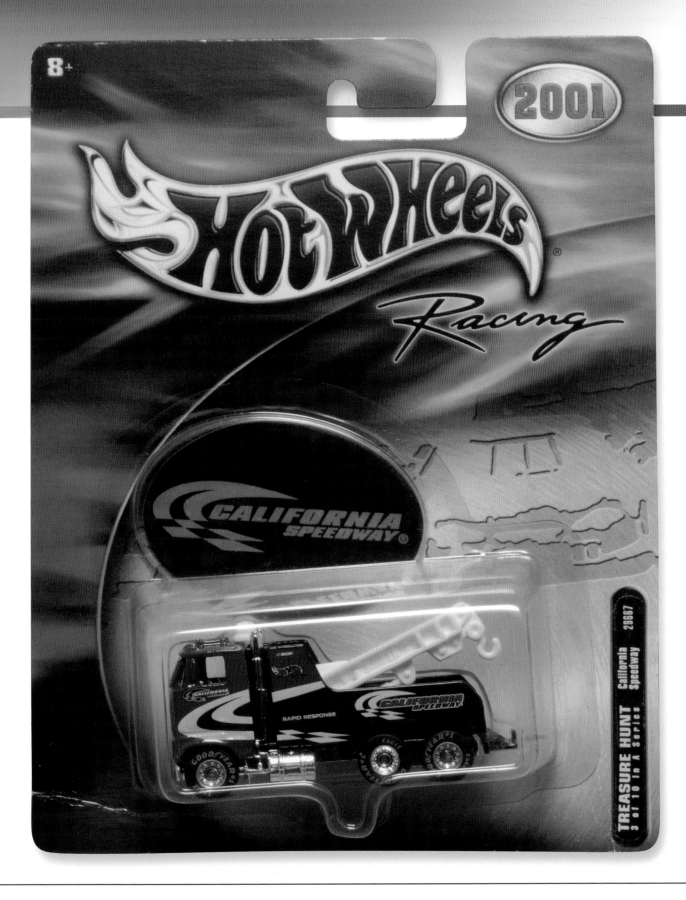

In 2001, the Treasure Hunt line was extended to the Hot Wheels Racing series. Every Treasure Hunt was based on a Rig Wrecker, and each of those 10 trucks represented a different racetrack.

'68 Cougar Treasure Hunt
from 2002.

'40 Ford truck Treasure
Hunt from 2002.

Ford Thunderbolt Treasure
Hunt from 2002.

Mini Cooper Treasure
Hunt from 2002.

Postwar Ford-based Shoe Box
Treasure Hunt from 2003.

Panoz LMP-1 Roadster S
Treasure Hunt from 2002.

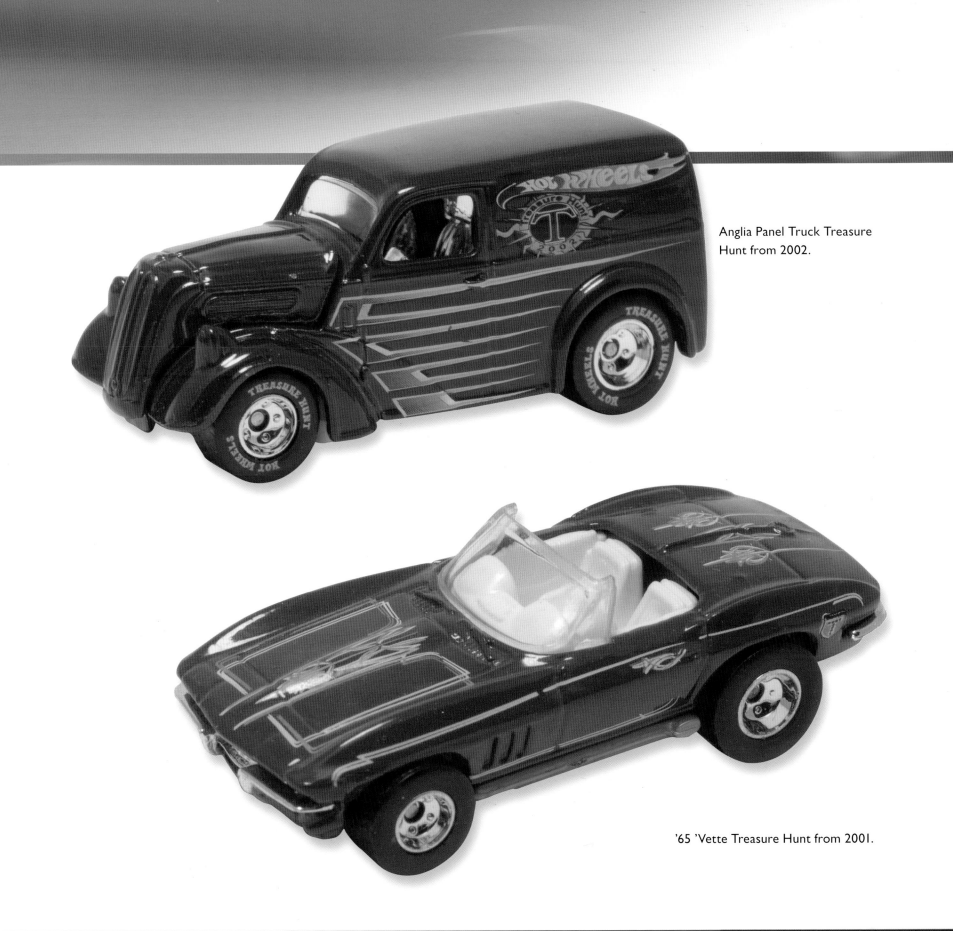

Anglia Panel Truck Treasure Hunt from 2002.

'65 'Vette Treasure Hunt from 2001.

La Troca Treasure Hunt
from 2002.

Fat Fendered '40 Treasure
Hunt from 2002.

Lotus Project M250 Treasure Hunt from 2002.

'57 Roadster Treasure Hunt from 2002.

'68 El Camino Treasure Hunt from 2003.

Midnight Otto Treasure Hunt from 2003.

'56 Ford Truck Treasure Hunt from 2003.

Hooligan Treasure Hunt from 2003.

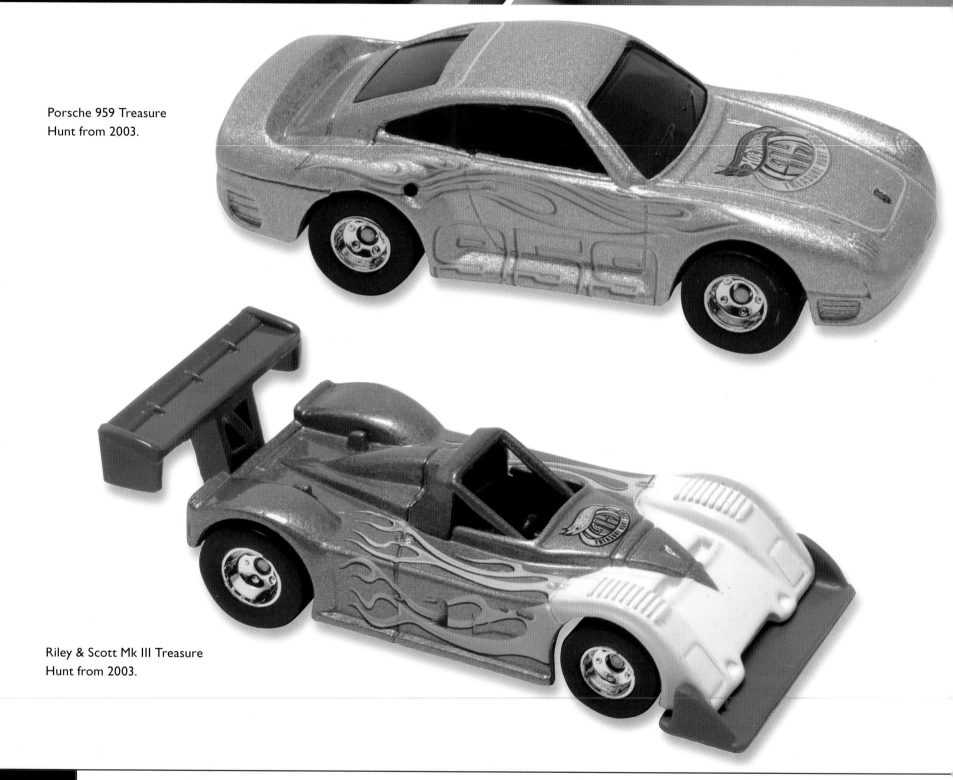

Porsche 959 Treasure
Hunt from 2003.

Riley & Scott Mk III Treasure
Hunt from 2003.

Dairy Delivery Treasure
Hunt from 2006.

'67 Mustang Treasure
Hunt from 2006.

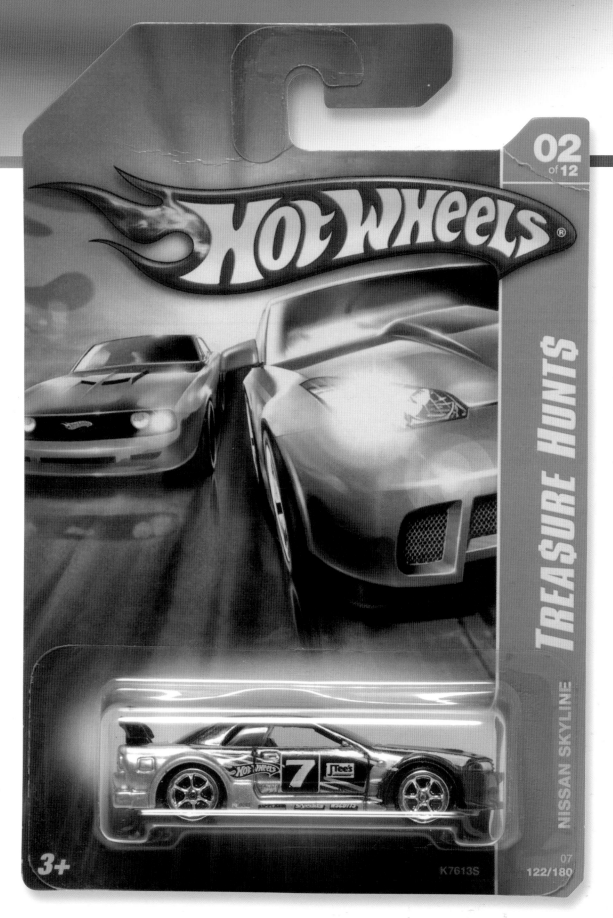

In a first for the Treasure Hunt series, there were two types of Treasure Hunts. A Super Treasure Hunt was aimed at the collector and featured low production numbers and synthetic rubber tires. A more common Treasure Hunt line in an identical or similar tampo and paint pattern was produced in larger numbers and with basic wheels in an attempt to help children find the special cars, as well. This Nissan Skyline from 2007 represents the more rare Super Treasure Hunt line with its synthetic rubber tires.

SPICING UP STORE SHELVES

Real hot rods are made from picking through the parts bin, and that looks like the process behind this 2007 New Model, Straight Pipes. It looks like a 1932 Ford Victoria body, Lincoln V-12 engine and 1933 Nash grille shell were used to create this wild car, which was then painted "hello yellow."

Back on the pegs, the 2007 Hot Wheels season started with a bang, and it went beyond new packaging and series names.

Ray Adler, associate marketing manager for 2007's basic Hot Wheels line, introduced the first new series of the year—"Code Cars"—and the initial model to be unveiled was the 'Tooned Dodge Charger Daytona in metallic green. Each car in the series featured a code printed on its chassis that could be entered on HotWheels.com to reveal more about the toy.

"The Code Cars series was designed to get kids excited about collecting, and drive [the kids] to the web," Adler said upon the car's debut.

Since this series was aimed at the young collector, it's not surprising that the youth-appealing casting was chosen to lead off the series.

"The idea of the code is that it will unlock some cool [online] features targeted at kids," he added, "such as a hidden level in one of our online games or wallpaper. And it will allow you to keep track of which of the code cars you have and which ones you don't. Each individual car will have a code.

"This, along with our instant-win promotion, is the first step in making www.HotWheels.com a car destination for kids," Adler continued. "We are unveiling a new mainline section [on the site] to educate kids about the fun and value of collecting."

The '70 Road Runner was offered in many different guises. Here, it's part of an Editor's Choice series with premium Real Riders wheels.

Pontiac's 1970 Firebird was given the Hot Wheels treatment for 2007. The toy version featured a smoother and bulkier body than stock, and an obviously more potent twin-turbo engine.

Although the Code Car series was targeted at making Hot Wheels cars more interactive with children, Mattel hadn't forgotten the adult collector. Adler noted there would again be a variety of castings—some appealed to children, but others grabbed the eye of the collector.

Changes continued down to the renaming of Hot Wheels' popular "first editions" series. In this Hot Wheels line, the cars were renamed "new models." In explaining the change, Adler said that while collectors were familiar with the Hot Wheels hierarchy, parents and children were not likely to understand the Hot Wheels nomenclature. To clarify the newness of the cars previously referred to as first editions, the name was changed to new models, at least in the United States.

"We will use the name 'First Editions' on our multi-lingual packaging in 2007, but we will use 'New Models' domestically," he said. "We felt the average consumer didn't realize first editions meant a newly tooled vehicle, so we changed it to something simpler."

Just because the Hot Wheels crew was making things easier for the public didn't mean they were making their own lives any simpler. The company quickly brought Detroit's hottest concept cars to the scale toy market.

New Model Lineup

"I think this is one of our strongest new-model lineups ever," Adler said of the 2007 New Models series. "We've got a good mix of the hottest new concept cars, such as the Challenger and Camaro, as well as old-school muscle, such as the '69 Mustang and '66 Nova. [We also have] designer originals and, of course, the Batmobile."

Not everything in the 2007 Hot Wheels line was so black-and-white. Hot Wheels cars in the new Mystery series were all black. Castings in the Mystery series featured never-seen-before blacked-out blisters that hid the enclosed cars' identities while on the pegs.

While the castings inside the blacked-out packages could not be determined, except by those deep within the organization, the Hot Wheels crew didn't want the cars to be a complete secret.

"The intent is not to make the cars secret, just to make it tough to figure out which car you are getting," Adler noted when the cars were unveiled.

Plans for this series began about nine months before their unveiling. Some of the castings included in the 24-car series were the '70 Plymouth Barracuda, VW Bug convertible and a newly tooled animated Batmobile. Some AcceleRacers models reappeared

Though popular with collector car owners for several years earlier, General Motors G-bodies from the 1980s were just catching on with toy producers in the 2000s. This Buick Grand National hit the 2007 New Models series with Faster Than Ever wheels, much to collectors' surprise.

DaimlerChrysler and General Motors hit the 2006 show circuit with hot new prototypes, and Mattel followed suit by casting them in toy form. The manufacturer's prototypes were later promised to head into production, but to make the wait easier to bear, these Hot Wheels versions were there to tide collectors over.

in the Mystery series, and production quantities of all Mystery cars varied upon the casting.

"Some [production quantities] will rival a normal basic car, while some will rival a Treasure Hunt," Adler said. "That's part of the fun of the series . . . not only is it a mystery which car you will get, we also plan on having the cars vary in rarity.

"I think collectors will have a lot of fun with this series, and I don't think these will last long on the shelf," he added.

Given the expected popularity and secretive

nature of the Mystery series, Adler tried to guess whether collectors would hold the long tradition of leaving their cars in their respective blister packs or break them open. "I think we'll create a lot of new people [who] are 'openers,' but I bet it will be fairly split between opening and keeping them in packages."

Not everything was a mystery in 2007. Mattel was clearly readying itself for a grand 40th anniversary celebration. It was shaping up to be a party that children and collectors wouldn't miss.

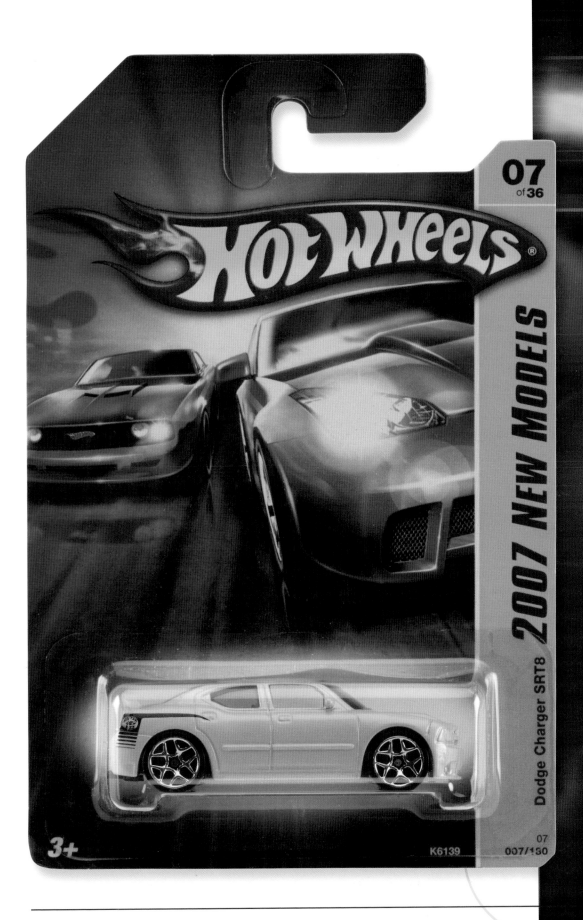

2007 NEW MODELS

Dodge Charger SRT8

3+

K6139

07
007/180

After calling new castings "first editions" for many years, Mattel began calling the line "new models" to help children and parents more easily determine which cars were new.

Many Mustangs had been offered in the Hot Wheels line through the years, but the new-for-2007 '69 Ford Mustang was given proportions never used by Mattel on a pony car casting. The most noticeable change is the chopped roof. Also notice the new Faster Than Ever wheels at the corners of this 'Stang.

One of the Mystery car surprises was a black version of the coveted '70 Plymouth Barracuda casting.

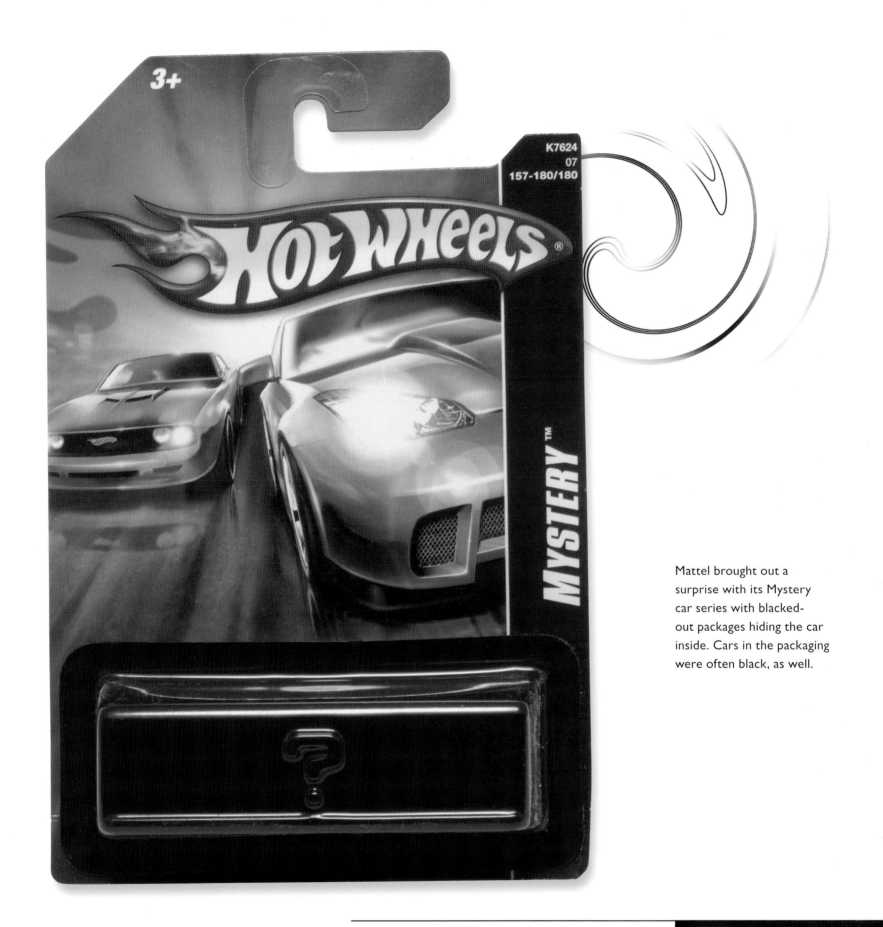

Mattel brought out a surprise with its Mystery car series with blacked-out packages hiding the car inside. Cars in the packaging were often black, as well.

As an ode to Ralph Nader, who is blamed for killing the Chevrolet Corvair with his book, "Unsafe at Any Speed," one of the Hot Wheels designers created this Corvair-based hot rod. Clues to the car's Nader connection can be found in the tampo.

For 2007, Mattel did something it had never done before—it offered two types of Treasure Hunts. Each of the 12 Treasure Hunts was given two different types of wheels to create 24 different T-Hunts for the year. The more rare T-Hunts were given Real Riders and other premium types of wheels, while the more common versions were given wheels from the basic line. Mattel's thinking was to give children a chance to find Treasure Hunts on store shelves.

Muscle cars regained much of their popularity in the late 1990s and 2000s, and Mattel met that popularity by offering an increasing number of muscle cars in its line, just as it had done in 1968. This '70 Plymouth Road Runner made a repeat appearance in 2007 as part of the Taxi Rods series.

The 2007 New Models series brought a new sheriff to town, and it answered to the name Rogue Hog.

Batmobiles trickled into the Hot Wheels line in the early 2000s, but by 2006, they were pouring. This Batmobile was hidden in Mystery car packaging.

CHAPTER FIVE Spicing Up Store Shelves

For the October 2001 Toy Fair, Mattel offered up this Ferrari Formula 1 race car, which was a mild work-over of a nearly identical, previously offered 2001 version. A driver-less cockpit in the Toy Fair version was the largest difference.

Hard to Top the Toy Fair

Toy Fair holds special meaning for Mattel, and it's an event the company attends and celebrates annually. Back when the prospect of Hot Wheels was still a shaky one within the walls of Mattel, and before one Hot Wheels blister pack swung from a peg at a toy store, Toy Fair gave Hot Wheels marketing the first inkling of its forthcoming success.

At the beginning of each year, toy manufac-turers, toy buyers and the media converge in New York City for Toy Fair. It's an event that offers buy-ers the chance to see what's new from manufactur-ers and to place orders for the toys they think will be the hottest sellers.

Mattel routinely holds a pre-Toy Fair gather-ing to offer its best customers a preview of what's coming. Through such previews, Mattel can weigh how its products will be received when the official event rolls around. It can also chalk up sales before Toy Fair even opens its doors. It was during one of these pre-Toy Fair gatherings that skeptical Mattel leadership first realized how big Hot Wheels cars would be.

Bernie Loomis, the head of Mattel's boy division, set up a huge presentation that filled an entire conference room in anticipation of unveiling Hot Wheels cars. His customer was Ken Sanger, the product buyer for Kmart, Mattel's largest customer. After giving his sales pitch and a brief demonstration to Sanger, Loomis halted his presentation and went straight to the point, asking Sanger what he thought.

Sanger said he'd take 50 million of the tiny cars, knowing full well that he could have ordered even more. Mouths dropped among Mattel's management, which included Ruth Handler, who initially figured she'd cut the company's losses short and only build 5 million cars, despite her husband's pleas for a production run of 10 to 15 million units. The order instantly created a new optimism for the brand.

Though the trade show was a springboard for Hot Wheels sales, it wasn't until 1975 that Mattel began giving away specially marked Hot Wheels cars to its customers and media members who visited its booth. The first casting to be given the Toy Fair treatment was the 1975 Super Van. The General Motors van-based casting was given special "Toy Fair 75" and Flying Colors tampo on white and chrome versions.

In his book "Tomart's Price Guide to Hot Wheels Collectibles," Michael Strauss estimates production of the Toy Fair 1975 Super Van to be in the 200-car range. For their rarity, white Toy Fair Super Vans fetch around $2,000, while chrome versions are in the $4,000 range.

The release of the Super Van in 1975 wasn't followed by another Toy Fair-branded car until the 1990s, but since at least 1992, Mattel has maintained the tradition of offering Toy Fair cars to the media and toy buyers.

Since the numbers of the hobby professionals there for each year's unveiling is relatively low, and Toy Fair cars are only offered at the event, collectors vie for any versions they can get their hands on, guaranteeing relatively high dollar values for any car that comes out of the February Toy Fair in New York. However, values for modern Toy Fair cars hover on both sides of the $100 mark, leaving them eclipsed by the 1975 Super Van.

Toy Fair-Branded Cars

2007 '55 Chevy panel truck with redlines

2007 Mattel Toy Fair Bone Shaker

2006 Split Decision

2005 Hot Wheels Classics Olds 442

2005 Pre-Toy Fair Blings Hummer H2

2005 16 Angels

2005 AcceleRacers Hollowback

2004 Hot 100 2 Cool

2004 Mitsubishi Eclipse

2004 Muscle Tone

2003 Hot Wheels Highway 35 Deora II

2003 Passion, black with whitewall Real Riders

2002 Planet Hot Wheels Protonic Energy

2002 Maelstrom

MS-T Suzuka

2001 Muscle Tone

2001 F-1

2000 Deora II

1999 Ford GT-90

1998 Twin Mill

1997 Kyle Petty racecar decorated Deora
 (supposedly Petty's favorite Hot Wheels car)

1996 Power Pistons

1995 Chevy Stocker

1994 Demon

1993 '93 Camaro

1992 gold-plated Purple Passion

1975 Super Van

The molds to create the revived Olds 442 casting hadn't been given a chance to cool before they cranked out three different versions of the casting: a gold Real Riders version for the Hot Wheels Collectors Club, red Larry Wood World Tour edition in a special four-car set and this blue Toy Fair version. Due to the lack of time between the casting's creation and its appearance at the fall Toy Fair activities, the tampo decoration from the Larry Wood World Tour version of the Olds 442 was reused for the 2005 Toy Fair version.

To bring attention to its Hot Wheels Highway 35 line commemorating the 35th anniversary, the toy company distributed special Deora II trucks with wild flames licking across chrome bodies.

To promote Planet Hot Wheels, an online entity of Mattel aimed at children, Mattel distributed this MS-T Suzuka at the 2002 Toy Fair event in New York.

A NASCAR-ready Ford Taurus decked out with Citgo sponsorship logos was given out at the 2002 Toy Fair event in New York.

Also given out to toy industry figures at the 2002 Toy Fair event was the Maelstrom in a patriotic red, white and blue paint scheme.

AcceleRacers, an interactive line of Hot Wheels cars, debuted in 2005 and coincided with a TV program on the Cartoon Network. To increase awareness to this line, an AcceleRacers Hollowback casting with Real Riders tires was given out at the 2005 Toy Fair event. A second Hollowback was offered on the shelves, but it featured co-molded wheels, like other castings in the series, and a different paint scheme.

For the 2005 Pre-Toy Fair event, Mattel gave out a chromed-out Blings H2.

Chapter Six

DRIVING THE DREAMS
OF DESIGNERS

Howard Rees designed the Mighty Maverick, as well as its Spoilers counterpart, the Street Snorter, which is pictured here.

They're the silent celebrities behind Hot Wheels designs. Their minds dream up the cars collectors covet, and their hands sculpt their images into reality. They are Hot Wheels designers.

If it weren't for the creative energy in Mattel's studios, Hot Wheels cars would be just another toy. But thanks to a long list of imaginative forces sketching and illustrating a sea of original and replicated four-wheel machines, Hot Wheels are the hottest toy cars on the planet.

Harry Bradley, Mattel's first Hot Wheels designer, started before the die-cast cars were even named. His designs shaped the essence of Hot Wheels cars, with the cars' aggressive stances, raked rear ends and overall sporty flairs, and these characteristics can still be found in many of the cars being designed 40 years later.

Shortly after the 1968 introduction of Hot Wheels, such known designers as Paul Tam, Ira Gilford, Howard Rees and Bob Lovejoy joined Bradley. But none of the artists can claim tenure at Mattel for as long as Larry Wood. Like many of the early Hot Wheels designers, Wood began his design career working for one of the "Big Three" car companies.

"I got out of high school and wasn't a great student, and all I wanted to do was draw cars and build hot rods," Wood said. "I was working at a company and realized that the guys next to me had

Howard Rees was responsible for the completely original Peepin' Bomb, which was built in the United States in 1970. Rees' interest in space toys is evident in this land-based casting.

Hot Wheels designer Paul Tam is responsible for Evil Weevil, a car from the 1971 Spoilers line. Cars in the Spoilers series took Harry Bradley's original design formula of raked rear ends, side pipes and other custom features to the next level.

been doing the same thing for four years. I went home and told my parents I wanted to go to college. The only college that would take me as a student was the art center."

Though he hadn't been a good student while in high school, Wood's ability with a pen and a clean sheet of paper helped him excel. From the art center, Wood earned a job at Ford Motor Co., and then headed for warmer weather in California. His next job was working at Lockheed Aircraft designing interiors for the L-1011 airplane. But it wasn't long before he was back working on cars, just on a bit smaller scale.

"I was working at Lockheed doing interiors

and was invited to a party at this friend's house," he said. "It was so foggy I almost turned around. I got to his house and his kids were playing with Hot Wheels. I remember the car, it was an Evil Weevil."

At that party in 1968, Wood met up with the supplier of the toy car, and it was Howard Rees, another ex-Ford Motor Co. designer. Rees was looking to get out of designing cars, and Wood was interested in the Hot Wheels car he had just seen for the first time.

"[Reese] said he wanted to work on space toys [at Mattel] and got me in, and they hired me right away," Wood said.

Another Ira Gilford design was the original Twin Mill of 1969, which spawned a full-size version of the car to be built and several modern scale Hot Wheels versions.

Not every 1968 Hot Wheels model came from Harry Bradley's pen; the Silhouette was an original design by hot rod builder Bill Cushenbery.

Several designers in Mattel's employ left their marks on Hot Wheels cars in the Spoilers series. Sugar Caddy came from the pen of Ira Gilford.

Harry Bradley's own mid-size Chevrolet El Camino custom influenced the first Hot Wheels cars, including Custom Fleetside, which he appears to have based on a full-size Chevrolet truck from 1967.

Here's Phil Riehlman's finished GTO. Although it's based on a real car, designers still spend a fair amount of their talents bringing full-size cars down to scale without losing a car's features.

The Head Noodle

One of Wood's first projects was to finish the design work on Noodle Head. Once completed, he dove into a project he had been aching to do since his automotive design days.

"My first car was the Tri-Baby," he said. "I had been working at Ford and never done a sports car, and never had the chance, so of course, the first thing I was going to do was design a sports car."

The sporty concept-type car was followed by other original creations, as well as toy cars based on full-size autos like the 1970 Oldsmobile 4-4-2 and Gordon Buehrig-designed 1937 Cord 812 Phaeton, both of which hit pegs in 1971. Not too long after, Wood found himself the only designer in Mattel's Hot Wheels studio, a state that lasted for more than 15 years.

"Elliot Handler would come by or stick his head in and talk," he said. "They did clay models at that time, and we drew pictures on the walls and actually sculpted the cars ourselves, sent them out and got models made."

During his tenure as the lone designer, change was minimal in the way Hot Wheels cars went from designs on paper to actual castings children could buy, but Wood did see an evolution in the legalities of creating Hot Wheels cars. The days of creating a 1:64 Chevrolet Corvette without getting licensing agreements from manufacturers were quickly ending by the 1980s.

In 2005, Larry Wood posed with his collection of 100% Hot Wheels models that he is responsible for designing.

"In the early days and up until we built the ZZ Top coupe (3-Window 34), we could create anything [without licensing agreements]. The ZZ Top car was the first legal problem," Wood said. "They called us up and said we had to work something out.

"The biggest problem is the legal end of it, where if you are doing a car of your own, there are no legalities involved. If you are not doing a one-off car, you need a long lead time, you have to send them graphics and models, and that's the biggest challenge," he added.

Mattel now seeks licensing approval for designs based on full-size cars, and enjoys good relationships with manufacturers.

"In the last few years, car manufacturers have been giving us electronic files [of car designs]," but Wood notes that the car designs need to be modified to fit the wheels and maintain the details. That involves the re-proportioning of designs to maintain details such as door handles.

The casting Larry Wood most enjoyed designing was the Purple Passion.

A Purple Passion

Of the hundreds of Hot Wheels cars that Wood has designed, his most memorable doesn't hail from the redline period or even the modern day; it's the 18-year-old custom Mercury-based Purple Passion that appeals to his hot rod side, as well as his designer side.

"For the first time, I could say the car wouldn't work on a track because the wheels were tucked under and because of the fenders skirts. It was the first time anybody said, 'Hey, collectors don't really care whether a car can work on the track.' It was a breakthrough," Wood noted.

Shortly before the Purple Passion struck store pegs in 1990, Mattel saw a surge in the popularity of Hot Wheels cars built for the 20th anniversary in 1988. As a result, the company hired more designers to help Wood create original and Detroit-inspired replicas.

The Hot Wheels design studio now includes a team of 30 people, up until recently including the talented Mark Jones, a senior project designer with such castings as Pony-Up under his belt. According to Jones, the current Hot Wheels design group is divided into four car categories headed by Gary Swisher, vice president of product design—Kid Sport, Kid Core, Die-Cast Trend and Graphics.

Designers divide their time working on Hot Wheels basic cars, collector cars and 1:18 cars.

"The day in the life of a designer is never the same," Jones said. "Typically, an average week would involve sketching and model building, attending team meetings, as well as overall discussion and coordination of design projects."

The way in which Hot Wheels cars are designed isn't the same, either. During the redline era and into the 1980s and 1990s, Wood used to find himself spending a lot of time "with a tape measure and a camera, crawling around the car." The procedure is still used on occasion to model full-size custom cars and other one-of-a-kind cars. To create the "Batman" TV show Batmobile for the Hot Wheels 1:18 line and basic line in 2007, Wood found himself underneath the original car in George Barris' California shop.

For other cars, the designing process is dominated by the use of more modern technology, mainly computers. But it still takes an artist's mind and traditional techniques to complete the process.

"Hot Wheels vehicles begin life in the imaginations of Mattel's designers," said Jones. "To keep up with the latest trends in the auto industry, the designers visit major auto shows, attend car racing events and study auto magazines for the latest on the cars of tomorrow.

"These creative ideas are then transferred onto an artist's drawing board. The designer may sketch hundreds of drawings as he conceives different ideas for a new vehicle. The best drawings of proposed models are then test-marketed with focus groups of children and adults," Jones explained.

Larry Wood went to see the original Lincoln Futura Batmobile in George Barris' California shop to create this 1:64 version for the Hot Wheels basic line.

This epoxy 1969 Pontiac GTO by Phil Riehlman is what Mattel refers to as a licensor model 1:1. It shows the final stage of how the metal body of the casting will look. The casting debuted in the 2005 First Editions series.

The Cast System

Approval for a new casting also comes through several team meetings and final approval from head designers. Once approval is gained, research begins to create a three-dimensional model of the car for the Hot Wheels line.

"If the vehicle exists in reality, photographing the original becomes the first step. Details, both interior and exterior, from close-ups of the grille, to overhead and full-length views, are captured on film. If the vehicle is a classic or an older model, manufacturers and owners are often consulted," Jones said.

"Precise measurements of the full-size original come next. Detailed dimensions, such as height, wheelbase and engine compartment overhang, are carefully noted. The photographs and specs are then sent to the engineering department where they are translated into mechanical drawings," he added.

Technology comes into play as designs are then converted from Computer Aided Design (CAD) data to surface files, which Jones said are used, along with the photographs, to replicate the rest of the car. Often, automobile manufacturers will provide the CAD files for their cars to Hot Wheels designers. "No dimension can be overlooked and every part and styling element must be in scale," Jones stressed.

"Next, the engineering drawings are sent to a pattern maker where a scale model is made. The model, which is four times larger than an actual Hot Wheels vehicle, is essential to make certain that all parts possess the fine, authentic detailing that has made the line famous," he continued. "Details are faithfully reproduced, including door handles, emblems, logos and the shape of a headlight or instrument panel. This realism is what gives the vehicles their unique look and personality."

Once a skilled pattern maker completes the model, its designer approves it as a pattern, and a die is made in raw steel. Jones said this process can take up to three months to complete.

"The final destination is the mold shop. The die-cast is injected into the molds and the body of the vehicle emerges. Next, it is polished and washed, and then spray-painted. Letters, logos and such detailing as pin striping are then printed," Jones related.

Inspiration for original Hot Wheels designs comes from all over. In the case of Golden Arrow, a 2003 First Editions model, its designer said it came from a coach-building firm. "My intention was to approach this design as if I were an Italian design house (a revived Ghia?) doing a modern Alfa-esque show car," its designer Mark Jones said.

Designer Mark Jones created Flight '03 for 2003 because he felt Mattel was lacking a car with a hatchback silhouette. "I wanted an over-the-top fender package and a lowered roof. If this were a real car, the wings could be attached to the hatch, allowing it to continue its function."

Classic cars were introduced to the Hot Wheels lineup in 1971 via the Classic Cord, designed by Larry Wood. Not everyone in Mattel was sure such a car would go over well, but the casting continues to be popular today and has inspired other classics to be included in the Hot Wheels line.

Born to Be Wheeled

Finally, all the parts, such as the wheels, chassis and engine, are assembled—and a Hot Wheels vehicle is born.

"The finished product is now a 1:64 scale diecast replica of the original vehicle," Jones remarked. "All that remains is road testing to Hot Wheels standards for quality and safety and creating a new name for the vehicle if it is not a standard production model."

After the body design is established, Jones said the designer provides direction to the Hot Wheels graphic team for the tampo decorations. Designers also select or make recommendations for the casting's wheels, paint color and construction. "These recommendations are then taken into consideration as the final touches and decisions are made to the vehicles," Jones noted. However, a designer does not create a casting's subsequent tampo decorations.

The designing process for creating a new Hot Wheels car is rapidly changing, especially in the last five years, because of the increase in computer technology. Now, the process of creating a pattern can be skipped, and designers can go from developing a Hot Wheels car on a computer screen in the CAD stage to making their own epoxy prototype at Mattel's El Segundo, California, headquarters without using the modeling process.

"Up until [five years ago], we made handmade models," Wood said. "Now, it's almost all computer. The coolest thing is that they send us files … and we can build a car here [through] SLA (stereo lithography).

"It can be assembled here, wheels, clear windows, everything but paint. Most of the guys send their info over the computer to Asia. [Prototypes] are plastic, but they are done in little layers. It looks just like a real car, but it's all gray," he noted.

Creating a new die-cast car is a rewarding process that involves a lot of time in an office, but getting in the field and working with people to build those cars can be equally rewarding.

"The most remarkable thing about being a Hot Wheels designer is sharing with other people what you do for a living and seeing their enthusiasm in response to it," Jones said.

"I have had several amazing experiences throughout my time as a Hot Wheels designer. For example, I enjoyed working with Rod Millen and having the opportunity to see his shop while I was working on a Hot Wheels version of his Pikes Peak Toyota Tacoma. And, during my time working on

the Chaparral 2 and 2D, Jim Hall cared enough that he went into his shop to make a template for me to work from so that I could create a more accurate version of his car," he enthused.

"There have been so many other wonderful experiences. I thought it was great when a journalist once told me that Gray Baskerville saw my Track T and said that it was the most accurate Track T he'd ever seen," Jones related. "I loved the fact that Luigi Colani, that purveyor of design wackiness, was amused by a couple of my designs. I also thought it was cool that J Mays [of Ford Motor Co.] wanted some Pony-Ups to send to his designers working on the new Mustang. And, I was gratified when Neko Publishing ran my story and illustrations of the Hyper Mite in its '2002 Great Pictorial of Worlds Miniature Cars.'"

With the talent, enthusiasm and imagination of designers like Wood and Jones, there's one guarantee for Hot Wheels cars' next 40 years—they'll be as hot as ever.

Hot Wheels designer Mark Jones came up with this original casting, which was in the Cruze series of 2004 First Editions. "LeMelt is a speed-stretched tribute to all the sensational long-tailed cars that have ever plied the Mulsanne straight," Jones said. "Phil Riehlman drew the very cool Ozz Coupe, and I was asked to do a vehicle in the same genre. So as a point of difference, I chose a more modern shape to torture on the tack of my imagination. Our mantra here at Hot Wheels is, 'Speed, power, performance and attitude,' and I'd like to think that you can hear the shriek of a multi-cylinder race motor each time you catch a glimpse of LeMelt sitting on your shelf."

For the latter part of the 1970s and most of the 1980s, Larry Wood was Mattel's only Hot Wheels designer. During that time, Wood created cars to fit every child's imagination, including this '35 Classic Caddy.

One of Larry Wood's most popular redline-era castings is the Olds 442 from 1971. To create the casting, Wood adhered to the 1970 Olds 442's original design but scaled it down to create this 1:64 casting.

For 1981, Larry Wood designed the '37 Bugatti, which is based on a Type 50 Semi-Prolifee coupe as styled by Jean Bugatti, a master at design himself. This version sports Real Riders tires as part of the Auto Milestones series.

Before the '55 Chevy Panel debuted in 2006, Ray Adler speculated, "This could be the best new tool introduced since the VW Bus. We believe this will be the only time [this truck] will ever be in the basic car line, and it won't last long."

A Hot Wheels design to come from outside of Mattel's doors was the Heavyweights S'Cool Bus. Tom Daniel created the chopped bus for Monogram Models, which Mattel acquired, along with rights to produce its products. (Tom Michael collection)

Because of their increased detail, the 100% Hot Wheels series gives designers more freedom, including adding low-rider-type suspension systems, like that on this Riviera.

A futuristic workhorse from the Ira Gilford-designed Heavyweights series is the Tow Truck.

This 2000 First Editions MX48 Turbo didn't come from a peg, but rather from Mattel's design studio. This purple casting is a Final Engineering Pilot (FEP), which helps finalize colors, wheels and other manufacturing choices for a casting. Most MX48 Turbo models came out in blue, but this casting was also available in purple, a much rarer color offering.

HOT WHEELS 40 YEARS

Oil can-shaped containers showcased cars in the collectibles series in the early 2000s.

Pending Release

For Approval

Toy Name : RAPID TRANSIT

Toy No. : B3543

From : KHAIRIL

Date : 9 · 23 · 2003

Rapid Transit, a 2004 First Editions model, was influenced by 1960s muscle cars, like the Plymouth 'Cuda, but probably helped influence the Dodge Challenger concept car DaimlerChrysler revealed in 2006. This is one of Mattel's "final engineering pilots," referred to as FEPs, and is posed with the paperwork. Such cars are the final step in the approval process before a car goes into production.

Larry Wood enjoys creating cars in the collectibles line because he can research the car right down to its details, like the correct wheels, interiors and paint colors. This '41 Willys coupe is one of the many cars Wood has designed for this series.

Ford requested several examples of this Mark Jones original, Pony-Up, for its own designers.

Here's a mock-up of what the packaging may have looked like for collectibles cars in 2005. The final package carried the same shape, but the colors were black.

Larry Wood created a 1:18 1959 Chevrolet sedan delivery, so he constructed this prototype 1959 El Camino in 2005 to complement it. Note the foggy windows.

Harry Bradley made many of Detroit's offerings even cooler by giving them sweet rakes, aggressive hood scoops and pipes sticking out the sides for the inaugural Hot Wheels line in 1968. His formula continues to be followed 40 years later.

Hot Wheels designer Dwayne Vance described this original design for Mercy Breaker, a 2004 First Editions model, as an expression of a Euro tuner. "Mercedes styling played a part in this car, combining it with the current tuner culture. I originally designed it with a single wing on the back, but after looking at the forms and lines on the car, I split the wing to make it more unique. It is a customized car that is built to the hilt with modifications — the only way a Hot Wheels should be built."

Some design projects take Hot Wheels designers into the field. Larry Wood worked with the original painter of the Hirohata Merc, Hershel "Junior" Conway, to perfectly match the original colors of the Hirohata Merc to the 1:64 Hot Wheels version in the Legends series. No other scale model of the Hirohata Merc carries the perfectly matched colors.

Hot Wheels designers sometimes take existing cars and then add their own twist; such was the case with Dodge Super 8 Hemi, a 2005 First Editions model. "Chrysler really wanted us to do the Dodge Super 8 Hemi, and I thought it might be a great car for the Drop Tops line," said Phil Riehlman, the car's designer. "I did a quick Photoshop sketch using an existing Chrysler photo to see how it would look. With its new thinned body section and roof, I thought it looked lean and mean enough for the Hot Wheels line."

Ira Gilford designed a line of futuristic heavy haulers for the Heavyweights line. Each casting shared a similar design for the cab, but the body varied depending on its livery. This Heavyweight is the Ambulance, but a cement mixer, fuel tanker and dump truck, among others, were also available.

By the mid 1970s, Larry Wood was the only designer on the Hot Wheels staff. Under his reign, original Hot Wheels cars hit the lineup, as did toy versions of popular full-size cars, like the Corvette Stingray from 1976.

Cars in the collectibles line have been decked out in many different packages, including this vessel that look likes it's from a mad scientist's lab. This vessel holds a '52 Chevy, designed by Larry Wood.

Hot Wheels designers toyed with proportions to create such series as Blings, Fatbax and Cruze series of First Editions in 2004. This FEP '70 Plymouth Barracuda carries its proportions well.

Sometimes, inspiration for designers comes from within Mattel's walls. The company's director of Hot Wheels adult licensing drives a '59 Chevrolet Bel Air, so to recreate his car in 2003, a new roof with a sedan pillar was added to the existing '59 Chevy Impala casting to create the Chevy Bel Air 1959.

Designer Mark Jones worked with famous race car builder Jim Hall to design the Chaparral 2D. The builder offered Jones cardboard templates off the actual car to aid the design process.

Designs got a bit crazy in an apparent effort to attract more of the Hot Wheels bread-and-butter audience — children. One of those wild creations was Slider, a slender sports car in the 2005 Torpedoes series of First Editions. Phil Riehlman designed the car and said, "I wanted to do a drifter style of car for the Torpedoes line. How cool would it be to see an open-wheeled car drift with all that smoke flowing from the exposed tires? Probably my strongest influences on the car were the Nissans, since they are key players in the current drifting world. Sketching and rendering are always the most enjoyable parts of the design process for me."

When his original car MotoBlade struck shelves as a 2006 First Editions, designer Mark Jones said, "MotoBlade was designed to be a great Hot Wheels track performer. It features a removable translucent body. This simple body form contrasts with the more complicated chassis, which is assembled from blades or vanes.

Phil Riehlman is responsible for this futuristic machine that's reminiscent of a redline-era Heavyweight. The casting featured a whistle built into the body with a visible fan blade in the middle of the body. To create the car, Riehlman said he "started with a bread board that utilized a whistle with a fan/turbine blade. The car was essentially designed around that bread board."

Larry Wood

From designer Larry Wood comes this selection of special cars from his personal collection. Wood, who has been with Mattel for more than 35 years, is, without a doubt, the toy company's most famous and most prolific designer. These prototype models and sketches offer a glimpse at the process behind designing Hot Wheels cars, from the first idea to the finished product, and range from the early 1970s to the company's latest and greatest castings. There's no question that after more than three decades, Wood's creativity has only become more exciting. Perhaps this is only the beginning!

This is a handmade epoxy model of Larry Wood's Classic Cord, which debuted in 1971.

Although dubbed "Hot Rod" when Larry Wood sketched this 1932 Ford roadster-based machine in July 1975, it hit pegs as Street Rodder in 1976.

This is a 1975 sketch of Jet Threat.

This sketch by Larry Wood
for a truck is dated August
25, 1982. The casting debuted
in 1983 as Long Shot.

Larry Wood's 1995
sketch for this casting
became Power Rocket.

The 700 millionth Hot Wheels car was produced in 1985, and here it is, the Hiway Hauler. The names of several Hot Wheels staff members decorate the box side.

700 MILLIONTH

1985

LARRY - DESIGNER
BOB - ENGINEERING
KENT - ENGINEERING
JOHN - PLANNING

GEORGE - AUTO ENG.
JOHN - AUTO ENG.
ART - PATTERNS
KATS - TAMPO

Here is an assembled 4-up (four times regular 1:64 scale) shell pattern of the '58 Corvette.

Shown are a first shot at
the Beatnik Bandit and
a handmade model of
the Power Rocket.

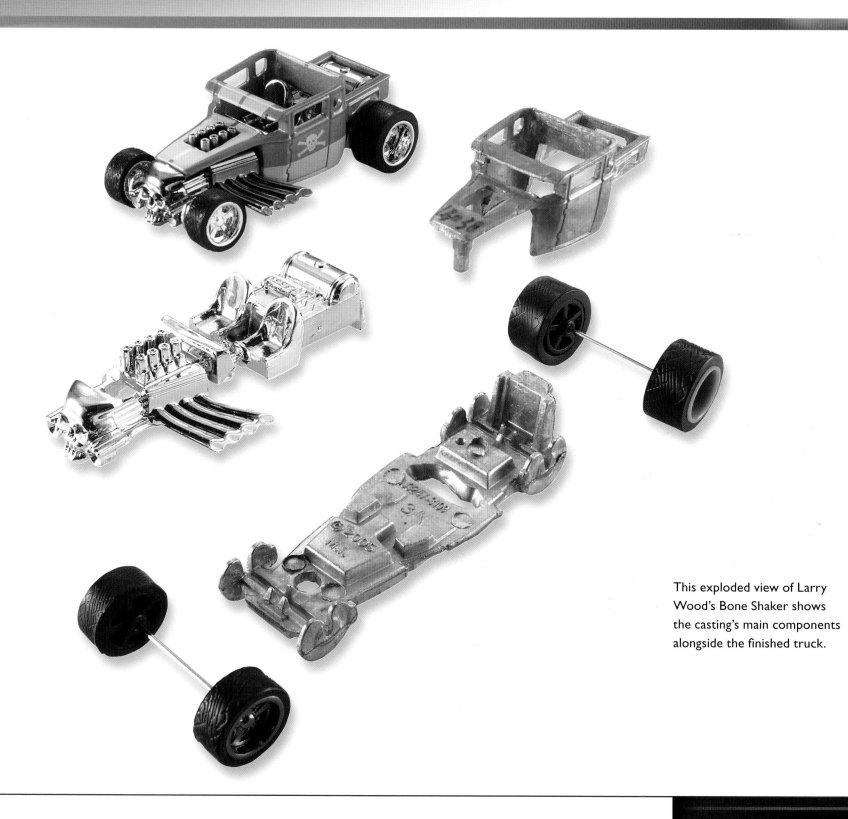

This exploded view of Larry Wood's Bone Shaker shows the casting's main components alongside the finished truck.

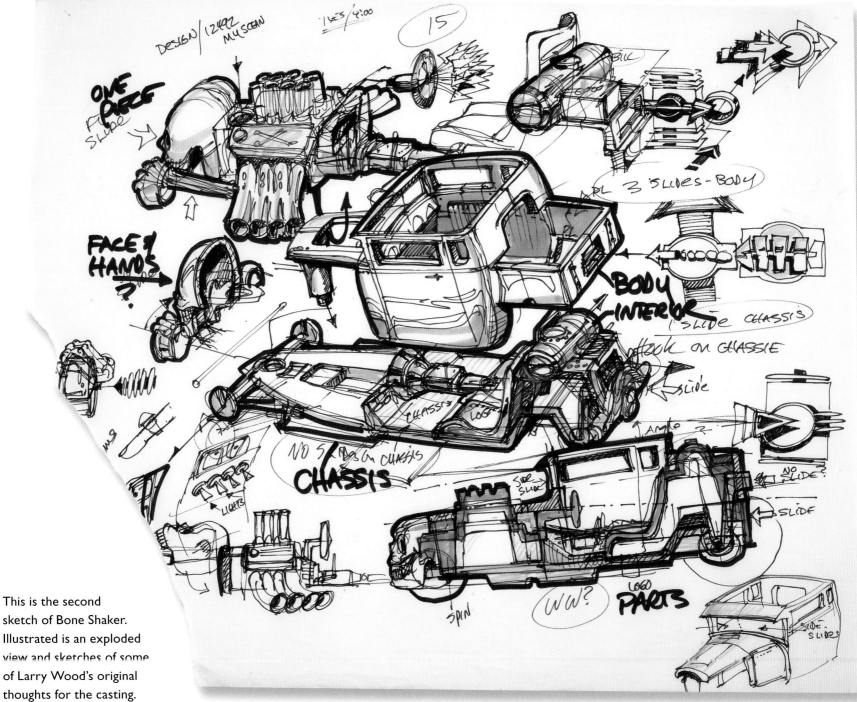

This is the second sketch of Bone Shaker. Illustrated is an exploded view and sketches of some of Larry Wood's original thoughts for the casting.

Paul Tam's 1971 drawing of Open Fire, a Gremlin-based casting, hit the pegs in 1972.

A 3-up epoxy model of Snake was the final model before tooling began.

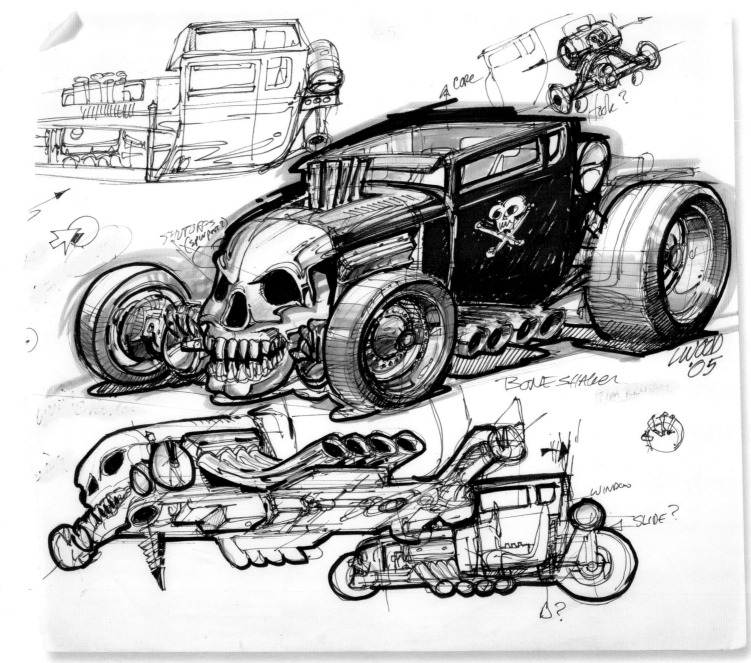

The initial sketches of what would become Bone Shaker illustrate Larry Wood's thoughts on how he could make it. The finished product was not much different from what appears in this sketch.

Here's what Larry Wood described as a three-up pattern of the Mercury Cougar-based Nitty Gritty Kitty.

Here is a 4-up wood pattern of the McLaren Can-Am Car.

These are first shots at
the '68 Dodge Dart, Evil
Twin and Pit Cruiser.

Pictured are painted epoxy
models for Toy Fair events—
the VW Bug, Red Baron
and Lotus Turbine.

Larry Wood's 4-up pattern was built four times larger than the 1:64 scale production version of the Ala Kart custom truck from the Barris four-car set. Note the lack of decoration on the mid-production version at left.

A 4-up shell pattern shows
the main parts of the
'58 Corvette casting.

These are what Larry Wood calls one-to-one epoxies, which are used for toy shows. Pictured are a '56 Flashsider, GMC Motor Home and '58 Corvette.

A 3-up epoxy model of Mongoose was the final model before tooling began.

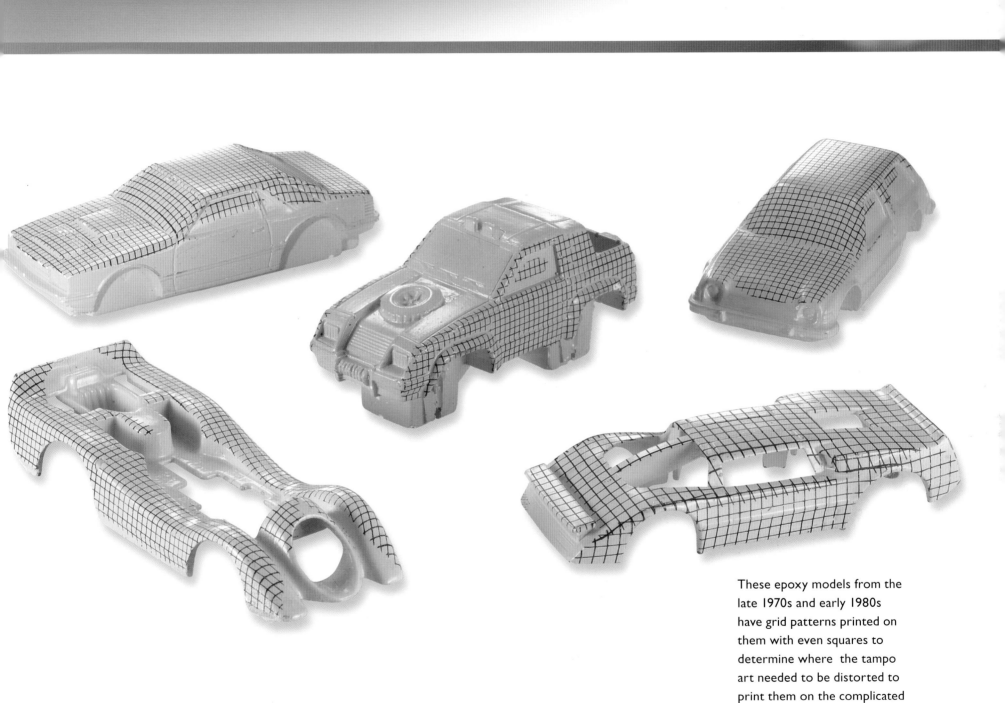

These epoxy models from the late 1970s and early 1980s have grid patterns printed on them with even squares to determine where the tampo art needed to be distorted to print them on the complicated Hot Wheels body surface.

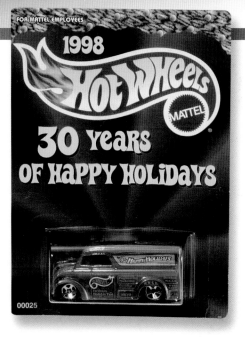

You've got to be a member of the Hot Wheels staff to get these Hot Wheels team Holiday Cars, and if you're on the outside, it's expensive to purchase them as production numbers are very low. Each hovers around 200 cars. This fun selection of cars dates from 1993-2002.

Chapter Seven

TOP 40 CASTINGS FOR THE HOT WHEELS 40TH ANNIVERSARY

One of the most coveted redline-era castings is the Olds 442 from 1971. Surprisingly, the "resale red" theory doesn't apply to this casting, as apple green and dark green versions tend to be more valuable than magenta versions, which are more common. This Olds 442 wears dark green paint.

The efforts of designers have ensured that every annual new Hot Wheels crop contains a selection that appeals to children, as well as to collectors. However, some castings stand taller than others in a field of winners and even gain a following among die-hard Hot Wheels collectors. Some Hot Wheels cars are less valuable because they are so common. Yet, more than 20 years after most adults last touched their Hot Wheels cars, when the words "Hot Wheels" are uttered, inevitably, a certain car casting comes to each individual's mind. This chapter recognizes those special cars.

Any "best of" list is subjective, and this list is no different. But chances are, every collector will find several cars that bring a smile to their face and, hopefully, pleasant memories to their mind.

Castings in this list are organized by their date of introduction, which often follows the copyright date on the vehicle's base.

1968

Custom Camaro

Some call it the first, some call it the most prolific model in the Hot Wheels line, but everyone calls it the Custom Camaro. This casting stands apart from the 16 first-year Hot Wheels models because many, including Mattel, considered it to be the first Hot Wheels car.

In its short run from 1968- '69, the Custom Camaro was made in Hong Kong and the United States, resulting in the typical variations associated with the two production lines. Some cars feature outlined doors and deck lids, as well as black roofs that simulate a vinyl roof. In 1983, Mattel brought back a very similar model—the '67 Camaro—and it remains popular to this day.

1969

Volkswagen Beach Bomb

There are many great castings from 1969, but "the bomb" among them all is the famous side-loading Beach Bomb. The popularity of this hippie machine eclipses other greats like the Custom AMX, Custom Charger and '31 Ford Woody from 1969, thanks in part to its rear-loading counterpart.

The Beach Bomb that hit pegs was the result of experimentation that proved the rear-loading version had too high a center of gravity and was too narrow to fit through the Super Chargers play set. Most collectors would count themselves lucky just to see, let alone own, a rear-loader, but the side-loader remains a good score in itself.

1970

Boss Hoss

Mattel pumped more muscle into its muscle cars with the Spoilers series in 1970, just at the height of the muscle car era. It also reserved one of those Spoilers for the Club Kit—the Boss Hoss. The casting was based on the Boss Mustang, one of the era's coolest cars, and was given a cool name to match.

The hoodless car featured an engine rising from between the front fenders, a stout rake and rear spoiler and a chrome finish exclusive to the Club Kit. The Boss Hoss was the first casting to be given out in the Club Kit, with a Chrome Heavy Chevy and King 'Kuda following.

1971

Olds 442

In a sea of offerings that teeter on the unrealistic and sporty side, the Olds 442 stands out as one of 1971's few street-fathomable toy cars. It's also one of few models based on Oldsmobile's most famous muscle car, which is just one of the reasons collectors clamor for the hard-to-find casting.

To create the casting, designer Larry Wood resized the 1970 Oldsmobile 4-4-2 to create the Olds 442. Many have claimed the model is based on the 1968 or 1969 Oldsmobile, but car collectors recognize the vertical quad taillights, as well as the headlight and grille arrangement of the 1970 model in the casting. For its accuracy and great looks, this U.S.-built car is the toast of 1971.

1972

Open Fire

By 1972, Mattel was catching up with demand for Hot Wheels cars, and building a heavy back stock of the cars, too. As a result, only five new castings were released in the basic line. Among them is Open Fire, a wild Gremlin-based machine in the long engine tradition of its 1971 predecessors Bye-Focal, The Hood and Special Delivery. The casting is found in only five colors and was only available in 1972, making it a coveted casting.

1973

Snake and Mongoose Plymouth Barracuda Funny Car

For 1973, everything was sprayed in enamel colors, and no other casting wore it better than the Plymouth Barracuda funny car. The casting was dressed up in four colors: blue, red, white and yellow. The Don "Snake" Prudhomme version wore white or yellow, while the Tom "Mongoose" McEwen came in blue and red. Oddly enough, McEwen drove a Duster, and the casting had been in the Hot Wheels catalog since 1971, though Mattel didn't use it for his car in 1973. There are other versions of this casting, but a valuable 1973 version has "6969" cast into the under side of the roof.

1974
Road King Mountain Mining Truck

Most Hot Wheels models were released in several colors, and later, with several tampo designs. But the Road King truck, or Mountain Mining truck, was a one-shot deal as it was only offered in the Road King Mountain Mining play set, and it was only available in yellow. And, it was only offered in 1974. All of these "onlys" add up to one thing, and that's value. The rare model is hard enough to find, let alone with its trailer, truck connector and dump leveler. Complete vehicles, and sets, can fetch nearly $1,000 each, in mint condition, earning it the pick of 1974.

1975
Super Van

Every kid had a flamed and black Super Van in the mid-1970s to early '80s, but not every kid had a copy of the more rare and far more desirable white, or gold or silver chrome Toy Fair versions, which were created for Mattel's accounts at the 1975 Toy Fair show. Memories are inexpensive for collectors who want to reclaim their youth through the black version once found in stores, but to nab one of the Toy Fair versions will cost more than $1,000.

1976
Street Rodder

Mattel went hot rod with the 1976 debut of the Street Rodder. This 1932 Ford "Deuce" roadster hit the scene in a black paint scheme commonly found on the popular full-size versions. Imaginative kids would pull the chrome plastic engine out of the engine bay for their own "backyard swaps," and in a nod to rarity, the car's inaugural year is the only one in which the car sported a set of redlines. After the United States' bicentennial year, this one would sport black walls or Real Riders tires.

1977
'57 Chevy

Counting all of its different color schemes, Mattel has cranked out more '57 Chevy castings than General Motors itself. After more than 30 years, Mattel continues to crank this casting out, and collectors of all ages continue to scoop the toy cars up as quickly as they can make them.

Initial versions of the red '57 Chevy feature smooth hoods with the double hood humps and chrome plastic bases, but some versions found themselves with blown engines poking through the hoods, and still others caught metal bases.

1978
Highway Patrol

It's not rare and it's not valuable, but that's all of its charm. In almost every kid's Hot Wheels collector's case, next to their Super Van, was at least one Highway Patrol, or one of its later versions (Fire Chaser, Sheriff Patrol or Airport Security). The Plymouth squad car origins of this casting are thinly veiled, which is partially why it was so popular with children. For its popularity, not its low value, the casting is one of the Hot Wheels top 40 castings.

1979
Auburn 852

Designer Larry Wood's affinity for classic-era cars (those cars recognized by the Classic Car Club of America) was just starting to show itself by the late 1970s. The third classic-era car to hit shelves was the Auburn 852, and there would be others to follow. The Auburn boat-tail speedster is a particularly striking car in full-size, and it held up well to downsizing under Wood's supervision. The car is so popular it hasn't ceased production since 1979, and most collectors hope it never leaves the line.

1980
'40s Woodie

Surf culture is still hot, and the '40s Woodie is just as hot. Whether people are deep into collecting Hot Wheels cars or are passive collectors, this casting invariably finds a place in their homes. The '40s Woodie was in good company—in addition to this 1940 Ford station wagon model, Mattel released the 3-Window '34, Split Window '63 and Stutz Blackhawk. The '40s Woodie stands out for its 24 versions since 1980.

1981
Old Number 5

Every kid needs a fire truck in his or her Collector's Case, and Old Number 5 more than fits the bill. This Ahrens Fox pumper hit pegs wearing an appropriate coat of red paint, and its bright, plastic work bits were plated in gold, reminiscent of brass-era of vehicles.

Considering its scale and $1 price point, there's a lot of detail and fun packed into the casting, which has only periodically sprinkled into the Hot Wheels line through the years. Collector demand brought the model back, though modified, in recent years.

1982
'55 Chevy

Proof that Hot Wheels designers are car people comes in the form of the '55 Chevy. Tri-Chevys, as 1955-'57 Chevrolets are called, never fell out of favor, and recognizing that fact, the '55 Chevy hit the pegs at the starting point of their enormous popularity. The first versions of this casting hit pegs with metal bases, but halfway through its 20 years, the '55 Chevy was given a plastic base. When scooping up this car, go for an early version with a metal base.

1983
'67 Camaro

Throughout the history of Hot Wheels cars, there's almost always been a first-generation Camaro in the lineup. It is believed to be the first casting, and count on it to always be represented. After the Custom Camaro's short run in the late 1960s, a Spoilers version replaced it in the 1970s. After a brief break, the Camaro returned for 1983, and it wasn't much different from the 1968 version. The casting was again based on an RS model, the hood still opened and it sported a metal base. This Camaro proves you can go back!

1984

'65 Mustang Convertible

The Hot Wheels line was built around muscle car castings, and another familiar face in the lineup was the Mustang. The first Mustang casting, the 1967 fastback-based Custom Mustang, was among the "Sweet Sixteen" original castings, but in 1984, Mattel went a bit farther back and captured the ever-popular 1965 convertible. The toy car model has been pressed out in a variety of colors, tampo decoration, and with nearly every type of wheel offered since 1984 in a true testament to its popularity over the past 20-plus years it has been swinging from pegs.

1985

Fat Fendered '40

There's no denying the great looks of the 1940 Ford, but the two-door sedan is often overlooked. Mattel didn't overlook it. The casting first hit pegs in 1983 as the Hong Kong-built '40s Ford 2-door, and then disappeared in a year. The casting sprung up again in 1985 with a new name and a new country of origin—Malaysia. Since 1985, it has been chromed, painted a rainbow of colors and given nearly every type of wheel known to the Hot Wheels catalog. The Fat Fendered '40 is also very popular as a premium car, and it deserves all of the attention.

1986
Rescue Ranger

Mattel dug back into Hot Wheels history and retrieved the Emergency Squad and Ranger Rig from 10 years earlier and dubbed it the Rescue Ranger for 1986. Other than wheel changes and different paint and tampo, the casting was the same hundreds of thousands of children played with in the 1970s, and with its reintroduction, many more children experienced this wheeled public servant. A Rescue Ranger by any other name is still a Rescue Ranger, and that's just fine with the countless children who associate this casting with sunny days on the sidewalk and in the sandbox.

1987
Ferrari Testarossa (not shown)

What Mattel does best is bring out the latest, greatest and hottest cars in pocket-sized toys with which children can own and play. When it made the Testarossa, it also placed the expensive Ferrari within reach of adults, too. Since its debut, the toy car has seen its share of paint, wheel and tampo combinations, some of which are very rare and command a healthy amount of money … but not as much as the full-size car.

1988

Talbot Lago

For 1988, the pegs were slim pickings when it came to new castings. Fantasy vehicles, animal-based castings and wild trucks aren't exactly what most collectors have in mind. There were a few bright spots among the new models in 1988, and one of them was the Talbot Lago.

The rakish French car must have been as unusual as the new Ratmobile and Radar Ranger, but it was and is a real car, and it's real expensive. There are a few rare versions of the casting, but even the common Talbot Lago models fetch more than their similarly common counterparts, a true testament to the popularity of the casting.

1989

'32 Ford Delivery

Unlike the previous year, there were several great castings to come out of 1989, including the Ferrari F40, T-Bucket and VW Bug. But the '32 Ford Delivery gets the nod not only because of its popularity, but its likeness to designer and car collector Larry Wood's personal ride. The casting hit pegs wearing street rod yellow paint with red tampo, and since then, showed up on pegs in many other color and tampo combinations. More importantly, Hot Wheels collectors often choose the casting for premiums.

1990
Purple Passion

It's not always purple, but there's no denying the passion collectors have for Purple Passion. When it hit pegs, Purple Passion was instantly collectible and highly sought. And its value hasn't wavered since. It's also one of the most frequently used castings for special edition and promotional versions in the Hot Wheels world, and people clamor for the casting just like the day it first hit stores.

1991
'59 Caddy

Again, several great castings hit the pegs in 1991, including the Ferrari 250, a new model based on the popular Mazda MX-5 Miata and the high-play-value Ramp Truck. The year also saw the return of a 1955 Chevrolet Nomad. But the car that gets the pick for 1991 is a boat-of-a-model, the '59 Caddy.

These barges were leaping in popularity, and Mattel was the first to get a modern toy of the fin king to market. Up until that point, toy 1950s Cadillacs were tough to find in stores, and as a testament to its popularity, the casting has been in more than two dozen paint, tampo and wheel combinations, including duty as a Treasure Hunt model.

1992

'56 Flashsider

Many collectors love 1992's Blimp, but many others collectors dislike it. Yet, they can all agree on the good looks and collectable value of the '56 Flashsider. By far, this is one of the most popular trucks in the Hot Wheels line, and in its short history, has been picked up in many sets and series, and has been used as a promotional vehicle for many companies. For 2007, its original designer, Larry Wood, added an opening hood, die-cast chassis and an interior—all items he's wanted to add since originally designing the vehicle.

1993

Olds 442 W-30

Mattel dug back into the archives to celebrate its 25th anniversary by releasing several of the first-year 1968 castings, as well as the popular 1963 Corvette split-window, but it was the Olds 442 W-30 model that nabbed attention. Like the extremely popular redline-era Olds 442 casting, the W-30 was based on a 1970 Oldsmobile 4-4-2.

Many saw the plastic-based car as a poor replacement for Larry Wood's original in proportion and construction. Yet, an Olds is an Olds, and this Demolition Man series product served its purpose by filling the hole left by the original … until the Hot Wheels Collectors version came along in 2003 with its opening hood, metal base and near dead-on looks of the original.

1994

S'Cool Bus

What was old was new again in 1994. Almost the entire line of new castings for the year were remakes of past cars—the Custom Mustang, Deora, '32 Ford Vicky, Snake and Mongoose, S'Cool Bus and Mutt Mobile. There were a few new cars mixed in, but they didn't find the following that the majority of other Hot Wheels castings found.

The crown of 1994 must go to the S'Cool Bus. The bus was rather difficult to find when it was released in the Heavyweights series in 1971, so its reappearance was as welcome as the last day of school.

1995

Ferrari 355 (not shown)

Everyone loves a Ferrari, and nobody casts more of them than Mattel. For 1995, the company added the Ferrari 355 to its well-stocked stable of Italian "prancing horses." The Hot Wheels staff works hard at keeping up with the coolest cars to hit the boulevards, and it was on top of the sports car scene. The casting debuted within one year of the full-size Ferrari's May 1994 appearance.

1996
Customized VW Drag Bus

Building the VW Drag Bus is like having a license to strike gold bars. No other modern Hot Wheels casting approaches the VW Drag Bus for popularity, or weight. This drag-ready Volkswagen-based casting is the heaviest basic Hot Wheels car to date, and collectors snap up every one that's been offered.

Mattel initially offered the casting as a 1996 First Editions model, but it hasn't been seen on the pegs with a $1 price tag since 1996. Its collector value remains high through limited edition runs aimed at collectors, usually with a $10-plus price tag, and Hot Wheels fans are happy to pay it.

1997
Scorchin' Scooter

There hadn't been a motorcycle in the Hot Wheels line for more than two decades, and demand for such a casting was clearly pent up. Hanging this bike from the pegs was like throwing candy towards kids in a parade—everybody fought to get one of their own.

Little has changed in the decade since the motorcycle hit shelves, with the Scorchin' Scooter maintaining its value and becoming nearly as valuable as its VW Bus predecessor. Interest in the Scorchin' Scooter encouraged Mattel to offer other motorcycle castings, such as Blast Lane, Dodge Tomahawk and W-Oozie, in the following years.

1998
Dairy Delivery

Mattel was on a roll by the late 1990s, offering great castings every year, and a lot of them. It's difficult to pick just one great car from 1998, but the Dairy Delivery stands out for its unique vintage design and its size, the latter of which makes it conducive to becoming a rolling billboard. Like the VW Bus, this model's roomy flanks made it a favorite among companies that used it as a promotion.

1999
'70 Chevelle SS

The pegs were smoking hot again with new castings in 1999. That year, Mattel released the '56 Ford Truck, '38 Phantom Corsair, Phaeton, Track T, 1936 Cord and, from the "Toy Story 2" movie, Al's Custom Cruiser. There were several others, but one of Chevrolet's most potent muscle cars, the 1970 Chevelle SS, joined the Hot Wheels basic line. For its introduction, the Chevelle received the coveted metal base and arrived in dark blue and gold. Subsequent cars featured a less-desirable plastic base, but all 1970 Chevelle SS castings are winners.

2000
Mini Cooper

It may be little, but the Mini Cooper packs more fun per ounce than any other casting from 2000, thanks to its removable body. With the click of a switch on the metal base, the body of the Mini Cooper pops off, revealing its plastic interior and other inner workings. Since Hot Wheels models were created with play value in mind, the Mini Cooper hits the top 40 list, squeezing by such other great castings as Muscle Tone, Deuce Roadster, Show Box, So Fine, Deora II and many other great 2000 cars.

2001
Hooligan

Mattel designers in the Hot Wheels division love creating entirely new and original designs—it's why they went to school. Adult Hot Wheels collectors tend to prefer castings based on familiar automobiles. These different theories meet in Hooligan, a circa-1934 roadster pickup given the hot rod treatment. The origins of the casting are clear, but there's no other vehicle like it on the street, at least not before this casting hit the pegs.

2002
Pony-Up

Hot Wheels collectors know how fun Pony-Up can be. Take it out of its package, then find the slickest, flattest surface in your home and push around this all-metal car. But before you fully release it along the surface, give the rear end a little English. The reward is the car doing a donut that looks like it's straight out of the movie "Bullitt." Designer Mark Jones is responsible for designing the Pony-Up, which strongly resembles an early Mustang concept car. For its fun value, it more than earns a spot in the top 40.

2003
Swoop Coupe (not shown)

Swoop Coupe is another Hot Wheels original that encapsulates what many custom car designers hope to achieve in their full-size autos. The casting encompasses everything that is good about fat-fender prewar car design—a Lincoln Zephyr-like silhouette echoed in each skirted fender, a pointed and deliberate 1937 Ford nose straddled by teardrop-shaped headlamps and a large trunk lid, also from the upper-class Lincoln Zephyr. Many great castings came out of 2003, but designer Phil Riehlman's long and low Swoop Coupe stands tall.

2004
Rapid Transit

Many collectors were left scratching their heads with the wild 2004 First Editions cars being cast out by Mattel. These unusual cars carried likewise unusual series names like "Blings," "Fatbax," "Crooze" and "'Tooned."

Several realistic cars kept the line grounded for traditional Hot Wheels collectors, but Rapid Transit went beyond satisfying old-line collectors—it predicted the future. Its svelte roofline, taillights and muscular proportions, as well as its lime green color and fade away graphics, all spoke Mopar pony car. Now, Chrysler is releasing a new Challenger, and it doesn't look too different from the Hot Wheels Rapid Transit. Usually, toy cars imitate life. Here, the toy is being imitated by life.

2005
'69 Pontiac GTO

Mattel offered a pair of "Ponchos" from the muscle car era, and both of them are striking cars, but the '69 Pontiac GTO gets the nod for its excellent proportions and attention to detail, right down to the "The Judge" graphics and stripe. Two colors were offered for this casting's inaugural year: black and orange. Collectors invariably seek the orange version for its similarities to the ideal Carousel Red version.

2006
'55 Chevy Panel

When it comes to play value, this truck has the market covered. The heavy '55 Chevy Panel has as many grams per fun as is possible in a Hot Wheels casting, thanks to its opening rear door. Once its rear door is lifted open, a bare metal motorcycle on a ramp can be pulled out the back of this otherwise unassuming toy truck. But that's not to say it's a mild casting—there's a lot to love beyond the truck's function.

Details keep the '55 Chevy Panel looking realistic, from the hooded headlights, which have been highlighted with white tampo, to the similarly highlighted parking lights. Even the grille and bumpers have been done exactly the way they should be: formed as part of the bare-metal base for the chrome-like look and the contrast against the body casting. Since it was produced in limited amounts, the desirability of the toy truck is through the roof and out the back door.

2007
Batmobile

Mattel took advantage of the opportunity to replicate, in toy form, the hottest cars to come out of Detroit—the Chevrolet Camaro and Dodge Challenger concept cars. But as good as they may be they still aren't the hottest offerings from a strong 2007 lineup of new models.

There was a new superhero ride in the Hot Wheels line, and it answered to the Bat signal in the sky. Yes, another Batmobile hit the pegs with all the "Pow" you'd expect. The fresh casting was a scaled-down copy of the car used in the "Batman" TV series of the 1960s starring Adam West. Even early in the year, the "Wham" effect of this car made it the best new model of 2007.

To build the Batmobile for the TV series, famous customizer George Barris took the 1955 Lincoln Futura show car, opened up the cockpit cover, modified the front and rear end and "Bang," the most famous Batmobile was born. The Hot Wheels casting was highly sought, making it hard for collectors to lasso. Those who did early in the casting's run were certainly superheroes in their friends' eyes.

Bibliography

Clark, Jack and Wicker, Robert P. *Hot Wheels: The Ultimate Redline Guide, Identification and Values 1968 - 1977*. Paducah, Kentucky. Collectors Books, 2003.

Leffingwell, Randy. *Hot Wheels: 35 Years of Speed, Power, Performance and Attitude*. St. Paul, Minnesota. MBI Publishing Company, 2003.

Ragan, Mac. *Hot Wheels Cars*. St. Paul, Minnesota. MBI Publishing Company, 2001.

Stearns, Dan. *Standard Catalog of Die-Cast Vehicles*. Iola, Wisconsin. Krause Publications, 2002.

Strauss, Michael Thomas. *Tomart's Price Guide to Hot Wheels Collectibles -- 5th edition*. Dayton, Ohio. Tomart Publications, 2002.

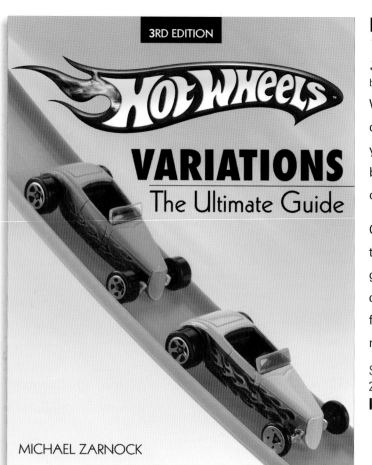